Ordering information: Quantity sales. Special discounts are available on quantity purchases by corporations, associations and others. For details, contact the "Special Sales Department" at pamc@pamelavcarmichael.com

LIVING SUCCESS PUBLISHERS

Published by LIVING SUCCESS PUBLISHERS

ISBN-13: 978-0-9917850-5-6 (paperback)

Printed in United States of America

TABLE OF CONTENTS

WELCOME!

I am so excited to be on this financial journey with you. It is my prayer that while using this workbook you will begin to experience financial empowerment. It includes exercises and worksheets that will address not only key money areas, but the spiritual and heart matters related to money.

The aim of this workbook is to move you into action—action that will take you from feeling overwhelmed or challenged by your financial situation to experiencing successes in your finances and in your life as a whole. The Lord God as a loving Father desires to see you prosper in all aspects of life, even in your finances.

I am not here to advertise any get-rich-quick schemes or to make you think that you will see results the moment you start applying these principles. This workbook is a starting point to your financial success, and certainly you will need to revisit it and reapply some of the principles outlined here throughout your life and financial journey. Just as it took time for financial challenges to develop, it will take time for improvements to become evident. Every day you are growing and becoming a better you. Through Christ you can become a better you in your financial life.

While using this workbook you will be challenged to examine your heart, your attitude, your relationship with Christ. Why? Much of what we do with our money is a reflection of how we view God and money and how we relate or do not relate to God.

As much as you and I might like to compartmentalize money into one self-contained area of our lives, we can't. For ease of understanding and for focus, you can consider that the main topic of this workbook is personal finance, but in reality money impacts life and life impacts money. In other words, your life is affected by how well you manage money and your money management is reflected in all the other areas of your life. For example, a health-conscious person will spend money to maintain good physical condition by buying and eating the right foods and maybe even on some kind of physical training. However, a person who is ill will spend money to get well by paying for doctors' visits, hospital visits (if any), special appointments and medication. In some cases they might even have to take time from income generation activities in order to get well. Someone who is sick will spend more money in a shorter period than someone who is well. Every aspect of your life determines the use of your money either positively or negatively. So throughout this workbook money will not be viewed in a vacuum, but as an integral part of your life.

Just as there are different areas of life, there are different areas of personal finance which intermingle with your life; areas including your relationship with the Lord. The purpose of reviewing the nine key areas of personal finance—creating wealth, tithing, saving, giving, investing, spending, borrowing, lending and planning—is to build a solid foundation for financial empowerment and growth in Christ. This workbook will help you to bring order to your financial life, learn what God says about money, and put you on a path to ongoing financial empowerment.

I know your personal finances are of great importance to you, but even more so to your Father God who wants the best for you. You would not be using this workbook if you did not recognize the need to put your finances in order according to God's purpose for you. Therefore, make the most of this opportunity. Invest the time and effort not only to read but also to apply the principles outlined. With God being your Helper, you will see a positive change in your finances and other areas of your life.

God Bless You!

To Your Financial Empowerment!

Pamela Carmichael, CFEI
Your Financial Empowerment Coach

YOUR FREE BONUS:
FINANCIAL EMPOWERMENT WORKSHEETS!

Before you begin, I have a free bonus to offer you.

This workbook is packed with valuable exercises and worksheets. As you start to work on the exercises, you may want to have them in fillable format so you can work on your computer. Moreover, since I want you to keep moving toward financial empowerment, I am going to share these worksheets with you. All you have to do is subscribe to my email list and I will send you the link to access them.

To receive your free access link please sign up below. It only takes a second. Go to this link to get the exercises and worksheets: https://www.pamelavcarmichael.com/resources/.

Once you sign up you will be emailed the access details to the worksheets. If you prefer to write, print the worksheets and place in a binder. Otherwise, you can save them to your computer and update them as you work through each section.

Enjoy!

To Your Financial Empowerment!

PamelaC

HOW TO USE THIS BOOK

I want you to make the best effort to complete this workbook and be certain that you have made progress towards financial empowerment. **Here are a few tips or recommendations to make the best out of this workbook:**

- ✓ Before you start reading and doing any of the exercises, please ask God for knowledge, understanding and wisdom, as well as the ability to take action on what you will learn.
- ✓ Get support. If possible, involve your spouse, friend or other accountability partner in the process by encouraging them to get the workbook and work along with you. You will have the drive to keep moving forward when you have the support of another. Remember, a three-string cord is not easily broken; working with someone else can be a great help.
- ✓ Take time to read each session of this workbook carefully. Sometimes we take it for granted that we know the scriptures or are familiar with the material. Please do not take anything written here for granted; the Holy Spirit is always willing to give new, fresh and greater revelation to us if we are willing to receive or learn more. Approach it with the eager heart of a child.
- ✓ Make sure to do the exercises in each session. The exercises are not just there because this is workbook, they are necessary for your progress towards financial empowerment. The aim of this workbook is not only to assess where you are now financially but also to help you get to and continually live financially empowered.
- ✓ Find the time that works best for you to complete the material. Reserve time each day or week to read and answer the questions. You may want to allocate time first thing in the morning or after dinner when family is engaged in other activities or when they are sound asleep. Whatever you decide, let others know that time is 'marked busy' in your calendar.
- ✓ As you go through the sections of the workbook, acknowledge what you already have in place and thank God. In addition, when you recognize that there is room for improvement, take action. Try to implement changes as soon as possible after completing each section; you do not want to feel overwhelmed with a long list after you have completed the workbook.

I hope these tips will prove beneficial to you. Remember to take one action at a time. Gradually gain insight into the areas you must correct or build up and be confident in knowing that you are making a strong foundation for financial success. You are well on the way to financial empowerment and I am cheering you on!

GET YOUR MONEY PERSPECTIVE RIGHT

It would not be right to start this workbook without first addressing some of the possible root causes to money issues you may be experiencing.

The journey to financial empowerment is not a singular event, but is an ongoing process and one that requires you and I to constantly evaluate ourselves through God's eyes and not our own, or not based on world views.

In the following two sessions you will examine your heart and your life in relation to your money. We will look at how your view of God affects your money, how your view of money affects your money, and how money affects your life.

Then we will deal in more detail with various aspects of money and managing it effectively.

Acknowledge the Source of Your Money

We need to realign our thinking and stop seeing God as limited in His ability to provide. Our thoughts need to be renewed through the Word to move us out of a poverty mentality into knowing and believing that we can prosper. A blessed man is a prosperous man.

— Pamela Carmichael, *Financial Empowerment*

It is perfectly logical to assume that a wise and competent Creator would provide for the needs of His creatures in their various stages of growth.

— Charles Fillmore, *Prosperity*

Knowing and believing that God is the Ultimate Source of everything you need in this life, money included, is paramount to you becoming financially empowered. If at any time you think that you— your job, your strength, your education, your family's wealth, your social status, even your sense of humor or ability to speak well, or anything else about you—has anything to do with what you have and or what you will earn in the future, then you need to rewire your thinking.

I don't think there is a finance book written from a biblical perspective or a Christian personal finance class or course that does not emphasize the importance of Who owns all that we see in this earth. The popular Psalm 24:1 "The earth is the Lord's, and everything in it, the world, and all who live in it," cannot be emphasised enough. Scripture doesn't even need to be quoted to emphasize this fact. The reality that we cannot and do not have control over the atmosphere is evidence of this great God. The fact that there is such an abundance on the earth—plants, trees, water, silver, gold, precious stones, etc—is proof of a God who took great care in providing for his children in advance of placing them on the earth to rule it (See Genesis 2). *Right now, pause from reading and meditate on that.*

Look outside your window or door and bask in the vastness of what is around you. The God who created this earth and created you would not leave you alone and impoverished, He cares for you too much to do that.

He who did not spare [even] His own Son, but gave Him up for us all, how will He not also, along with Him, graciously give us all things? – Romans 8:32 (AMP)

Identify Your Limiting Beliefs

Now that you're back and have taken time to reflect on the abundance around you. Consider these questions:

- Has there ever been a time when you focused so much on working hard to provide for yourself that you forgot to give thanks to the One who gave you strength to do it?
- Was there a time when you were so proud of your accomplishments in life—financial or otherwise—that you forgot who caused your successes to be?
- Have you worried constantly when you didn't have enough and you couldn't see where the money was going to come from to pay the bills or to feed you and your family, or make ends meet in some way?

As you think about those scenarios, can you pinpoint why you didn't believe God would have provided for you then? Or to ask it another way: What are some of the limiting beliefs you have about God's provision for you?

Here are some limiting belief statements. Check the ones that apply to you.
- ☐ I don't believe that God wants me to prosper.
- ☐ I have tried new things—career, business—but deep down inside I doubt that I'd be

    successful and usually that's what happens.

☐ If God wants me to prosper, why am I struggling so much?

☐ As much as the Bible says that the Lord will provide all my needs, I still don't see it and it's hard to believe especially when I have unmet needs.

☐ When challenging times come I have difficulty keeping my faith in God to provide.

☐ I worry a lot. I worry whether there is enough for now and for the future.

☐ I try to find solutions to my financial challenges and often end up feeling frustrated or in deeper trouble than I was before. I am not sure what else to do.

☐ I see people succeeding, especially unbelievers, but I don't see that happening to me!

☐ My family has always struggled financially and I don't seem to be doing any better than they are.

☐ It's up to me. I work hard and I think I am quite capable of taking care of my family and myself.

☐ I don't think financial prosperity is for everyone. I am content with the little I have so let's leave it at that.

☐ I figure the only way God provides is through my work, I don't see Him taking care of me by any other means.

☐ I used to dream of doing great things with my life, but now I am not sure God wants me to fulfill those dreams.

☐ Jesus said it, that there would always be poor people in the world, so I guess I am seen as one of the poor.

Did I miss anything? What other reasons not listed above can you identify? Write out any other limiting thoughts about God's provision for you.

_____

_____

_____

_____

_____

_____

_____

_____

_____

Learn to Trust God

Do you know what the word 'source' means? I am sure you must be saying "Of course I do." I know you do, but I want to reiterate it here. It is important to keep this in mind since it determines not only your internal perspective towards money and how you manage it, but also the impact on your finances—increase vs. decrease, struggle vs success. Therefore, always remember this: God is your Source. By definition God is the Creator, the Originator, the Sustainer, and the Father of all Creation. Wow! Do you get that? Therefore since your God is ALL THAT, as His child, what you have got to worry about? I would hope your answer is "Nothing at all." ☺

The previous exercise may have proven a bit challenging and hopefully eye-opening for you as you identified more clearly for yourself the underlying issues that are affecting your ability (1) to trust God for who His is and Who the Bible says He is and (2) to be an effective manager of your finances.

To combat and destroy the strongholds that have affected your life up until now, I want you to dig deep into the word of God to feed and feast yourself—your spirit, soul and body—on the Bread of Life that has the power to change the way you feel, think and act towards God as it relates to money.

For each of the limiting beliefs identified above, I have indicated a scripture to address it. In some cases I have also inserted a 'Confession of Faith'. However, I leave it up to you to speak life into your finances in your own way.

As you read these scriptures let them penetrate into your hearts. It has been said over and over again that what a man thinks in his heart, he becomes (Prov. 23:7) and the Apostle Paul encourages us to think on good things (Phil. 4:8). Take time daily to focus on these words of life and not only read but also connect these scriptures to yourself. You can even write out these scriptures on an index card and save them in your cell phone so you can easily retrieve them and meditate on or say them repeatedly. This will help you not just to know what the word of God says, but to grow in faith as you hear yourself speak it.

So faith comes from hearing [what is told], and what is heard comes by the [preaching of the] message concerning Christ.

— Romans 10:17 (AMP)

Limiting belief	Scripture	Confession of faith
I don't believe that God wants me to prosper.	*He shall be like a tree planted by the rivers of water that brings forth its fruit in its season, whose leaf also shall not wither; and whatever he does shall prosper.* — Psalm 1:3	I am a blessed person and whatever I do will prosper
I have tried new things – career, business – but deep down inside I doubt that I'd be successful and usually that's what happens.	*Commit your works to the Lord [submit and trust them to Him],* *And your plans will succeed [if you respond to His will and guidance].* — Prov. 16:3 (AMP)	
If God wants me to prosper, why am I struggling so much?	*Beloved, I pray that you may prosper in all things and be in health, just as your soul prospers.* — 1 John 1:2	*God desires for me to prosper and be in good health just as much as He desires my relationship with Him to thrive*
As much as the Bible says that the Lord will provide all my needs, I still don't see it and it's hard to believe, especially when I have unmet needs.	*And my God shall supply all your need according to His riches in glory by Christ Jesus.* — Phil. 4:19	

Limiting belief	Scripture	Confession of faith
When challenging times come I have difficulty keeping my faith in God to provide.	*So faith comes from hearing [what is told], and what is heard comes by the [preaching of the] message concerning Christ.* — Romans 10:17 (AMP)	
I worry a lot. I worry whether there is enough for now and for the future.	*Be anxious for nothing, but in everything by prayer and supplication, with thanksgiving, let your requests be made known to God;* *7 and the peace of God, which surpasses all understanding, will guard your hearts and minds through Christ Jesus.* — Phil. 4:6-7	I won't worry about anything. I will give thanks to God and ask Him to take care of me.
I try to find solutions to my financial challenges and often end up feeling frustrated or in deeper trouble than I was before. I am not sure what else to do.	*Trust in and rely confidently on the Lord with all your heart and do not rely on your own insight or understanding. In all your ways know and acknowledge and recognize Him, and He will make your paths straight and smooth [removing obstacles that block your way].* — Prov. 3:5-6 (AMP)	I must first seek God before stepping out to do anything. I will seek His guidance instead of others, especially those not in Christ, to help me make the right choices.

Limiting belief	Scripture	Confession of faith
I see people succeeding, especially unbelievers, but I don't see that happening to me!	*Rest in the Lord, and wait patiently for Him; Do not fret because of him who prospers in his way, Because of the man who brings wicked schemes to pass.* — Psalm 37:7	
My family has always struggled financially and I don't seem to be doing any better than they are.	*And my God shall supply all your need according to His riches in glory by Christ Jesus.* — Phil. 4:19	My God will supply – richly fill, satisfy, copiously supply, abundantly supply, plentifully supply, fully supply, liberally supply, fill to the full – every one of my needs.
It's up to me. I work hard and I think I am quite capable of taking care of myself and my family.	*But you shall remember [with profound respect] the Lord your God, for it is He who is giving you power to make wealth.* — Deut. 8:18a	
I don't think financial prosperity is for everyone. I am content with the little I have, so let's leave it at that.	*Beloved, I pray that in every way you may succeed and prosper and be in good health [physically], just as [I know] your soul prospers [spiritually].* — 3 John 2 (AMP)	

Limiting belief	Scripture	Confession of faith
I figure the only way God provides is through my work, I don't see Him taking care of me by any other means.	*However, so that we do not offend them, go to the sea and throw in a hook, and take the first fish that comes up; and when you open its mouth, you will find a shekel. Take it and give it to them* [to pay the temple tax] *for you and Me.* — Read Matt. 17:24-27	Lord, may I not have in-the-box thinking anymore. If you can provide money through a fish's mouth, you can use any means to provide for me!
I used to dream of doing great things with my life, but now I am not sure God wants me to fulfill those dreams.	*For I know the plans and thoughts that I have for you,' says the Lord, 'plans for peace and well-being and not for disaster, to give you a future and a hope.* —Jer. 29:11 (AMP)	
Jesus said it, that there would always be poor people in the world, so I guess I am counted as one of the poor.	*I was young and now I am old, yet I have never seen the righteous forsaken or their children begging bread.* — Psalm 37:25 (NIV)	

At the end of this exercise and on a consistent basis, your daily confessions should be summed up like this:

- ☐ I trust God completely. I know He takes care of me. I pray and study the Word and seek the counsel of strong Christians to get His direction for my life including my finances.
- ☐ By His power, God has provided everything I need to enjoy life and to live upright before Him.

As His divine power has given to us all things that pertain to life and godliness, through the knowledge of Him who called us by glory and virtue. — 2 Peter 1:3

Take a Walk – Exercise

Anytime you feel financially boxed-in or you think that God is limited in His ability to help you, take a walk or go for a ride in your car. Look up at the sky and view the vast scenery around you. Does anything seem lacking? The Painter of the sky, the Creator and Designer of the earth, is your Father. If He so fittingly provided for this earth and the many billions of people who live in it, then remind yourself that He has provided for you. God is your Source.

Time for a Reset

God is an amazingly loving Father. Learning about any limiting beliefs you may have had about God care for you and His ability to provide was not meant to make you feel bad. Of course, not! This section was designed to help you press the reset button or to restart your financial life with Christ at the helm. This is a time for you to develop confidence in the word of God and the God Himself. It is time to have faith in God – who He is – and believe that His is both willing and very capable of taking care of you.

Throughout the workbook, I will ask you to pray about specific financial areas and related issues you undercover in the process. However, you can start right now – ask God to help you renew your mind and heart and forgive you for any negative thoughts so you can live financial empowered through Him.

Let's move on and dig a little deeper into money matters.

LOOK DEEP INTO THE
HEART OF MONEY MATTERS

"For money to be a valuable resource, you must master it, see its usefulness and use it effectively."

— Pamela Carmichael, *Financial Empowerment*

You've bought this workbook for a reason. Most likely, you believe that it's time to get a handle on your money. This is a good move; a good decision. I applaud you for taking the time and effort to work through this. So far we've focused on the Source of all good things (including money)—God the Creator and Sustainer. Now we are going to do some more soul digging. Before we even get started with the numbers, let's talk about what goes on behind closed doors. Let's talk about how money impacts you emotionally.

Money is personal. Not only does it affect your bank account but it affects your emotions, your outlook on life and how you perceive others including your loved ones. Think about this: If you were to inherit a large sum of money, how would you feel? I am sure you would be elated and not to mention relieved because you have some extra that you can use to do some good, like pay off debts, purchase a house or even take the family on a long desired vacation. On the other hand, if you were to incur a big expense or lose big on your investments, how would you feel? Yes, the feeling anyone would have is worry or stress over how you can deal with that kind of financial setback.

Admittedly, we all experience highs and lows in our emotions based on how things are going financially. Sadly, most of us are stressed because of constant money woes. Financial challenges are known to be the cause of stress-related illnesses due to lack of self-care or much-needed health care, failed marriages, stressed children in families facing financial struggles, poor job productivity, and more.

Identify Your Mone'motions

In this section, you will identify money-related emotions (Mone'motions) that impact how your manage money as well as your wellbeing—spiritual, emotional, mental and physical.

The world places much emphasis on money. The fact is, you cannot do much without the currency. Therefore, you need to be aware of its impact on your emotions—your **Mone'motions**. Ask yourself the following questions to determine areas of concern in your financial life and where money may be controlling you in some way. Be true to yourself and give honest responses. The more you learn about your mone'motions the better you can master money rather than money control you.

How do you feel when you have to pay the bills?

_____
_____
_____
_____
_____
_____
_____
_____
_____
_____

What kind of reaction do you have when there isn't enough to cover an unexpected expense?

_____
_____
_____
_____
_____
_____
_____
_____

When there isn't enough money to make it through the month what do you do (e.g. worry constantly, stay awake at night, pray for wisdom on how to manage, etc.)?

_____
_____
_____
_____
_____

_____

_____

_____

_____

Do you identify with this statement: "Money makes my brain hurt!" What is your interpretation of this statement?

_____

_____

_____

_____

_____

_____

_____

How often do your review your finances? How does having to do this make you feel about your money?

_____

_____

_____

_____

_____

_____

_____

_____

Excellent! Good work in completing that exercise. Now, let us see how these mone'motions have been identified in the Bible and how you can overcome them.

Mon'Emotions Identified in the Word of God

"What's your love-affair with money?" This question conjures up at least two reactions: one of curiosity and another of disgust because of course the first reaction is that no one should love money. Even the Bible highlights that individuals can have an emotional connection to money. The unfortunate reality is that money can be such a strong force that we often form a love-hate relationship with it. Your response to money can either be negative or positive.

NEGATIVE RESPONSE TO MONEY	POSITIVE RESPONSE TO MONEY
• Love	• Hate
• Loyal	• Despise
• Worry	• Peaceful
• Greedy	• Generous
• Unwise	• Smart

Review these scriptures and indicate the emotional responses to money in each of them.

BIBLE REFERENCES	EMOTIONAL RESPONSES
No servant can serve two masters; for either he will hate the one and love the other, or else he will be loyal to the one and despise the other. You cannot serve God and mammon. — Luke 16:13 (also Matt. 6:24)	
Jesus' word of encouragement to avoid negative emotions – Matthew 6: 25-34	
And everyone who was in distress, everyone who was in debt, and everyone who was discontented gathered to him. So he became captain over them. And there were about four hundred men with him. — 1 Sam. 22:2	
Elisha vs. Gehazi's response to the gift offered –2 Kings 5:15-27	
The Parable of the Lost Son – Luke 15:11-32	
The Parable of the Rich Fool – Luke 12:13-21	
Jesus Counsels the Rich Young Ruler – Matthew 19:16-30 (also Mark 10:17-31, Luke 18:18-29)	

There was a certain man in Caesarea called Cornelius, a centurion of what was called the Italian Regiment, a devout man and one who feared God with all his household, who gave alms generously to the people, and prayed to God always. – Acts 10:1-2	
The Parable of the Unjust Servant – Luke 16:1-12	

YOUR LIFE & MONEY CONNECTION

Life happens. That is a phrase we often hear and yes, it is true. In the life happening, money also happens. Either money is something you avoid talking about and don't like to deal with or money is managed by you effectively or you have a neither-here-nor-there attitude about it. Whatever the response, money happens in the midst of life.

Unfortunately, any negative attitude or emotion to money leads to bad money management that results in negative returns: excessive spending and borrowing. This creates a spiraling effect that brings on more negative feelings about money. You freeze instead of dealing with money matters, hoard excessively, fear losing money or being in want, think limitedly about your ability to earn a greater level of income and so on.

However, you need to combat those negative mon'emotions so you can be free to effectively manage your money. In the previous exercise you looked at mon'emotions identified in the Bible. In this section, you will examine your life journey to see where you may have developed any negative emotions towards money.

Your Money Story: Unpleasant Events

What past experiences have left the proverbial bad taste in your mouth or have hindered you from managing effectively and making timely money decisions? For example, as a child did your family have money struggles or did you make a mistake that cost you a great deal financially and maybe even relationally?

_____

_____

_____

_____

_____

_____

_____

_____

_____

_____

_____

Your Money Influencers

What did you learn from your parents or teachers either directly or indirectly that has a negative impact on your view and management of money today? For example, "Money doesn't grow on trees" was a statement often said to children to deter them from asking for anything too pricey or out of frustration when money was limited.

_____

_____

_____

_____

_____

_____

What money practice or money perspective do you have now that is a result of your upbringing?

_____

_____

_____

_____

_____

_____

Your Perception of People and Yourself

We can often make judgments about people without really knowing them. Your preconceived ideas of how someone else makes or manages money (compared to you) is a reflection of your relationship with money. Right now in your life, who do you think has more money than you or seems to be getting ahead faster than you (e.g. co-workers, neighbours, your close friend)? What makes you think of people in that way?

_____

_____

_____

_____

_____

_____

Sometimes you might even have a low view of yourself. For example, you might quickly accept a low salary for a new job and not ask for the amount the position requires. Or as a business owner you might find yourself bidding low on a contract hoping that you would win it. Do you ever think you can earn more than you currently do? How do you feel when thinking like this?

_____

_____

_____

_____

_____

_____

_____

Your Lifestyle: Current and Future

Life goals, lifestyle choice, current income and your perceived or projected income and expense levels influence how you manage your resources. What other influences in your life have impacted how you manage your money? For example, consider how your co-workers, your neighbours, family members and friends have influenced you financially.

_____

_____

_____

_____

_____

_____

_____

Along with the immediate influences, there are others to consider. What has the impact of the internet, social media and advertising from various forms such as magazines, radio, and television been on your view of money and how you use money?

_____

_____

_____

_____

_____

_____

_____

Master Your Emotions & Your Money

Now that you have identified the money-heart issues you have experienced or are experiencing, we are going to move forward to overcome them.

There are several steps that you can take to get the emotions out of money and take control of your finances. I will address them in brief here, and as you continue through the workbook, these steps will be highlighted in different areas.

Let God Master You and Your Money

We've already talked about God being your Source. Definitively knowing who the Source is puts you in a position of being a good steward. Along with this, give your love to God, be loyal to Him and serve Him only.

Make a commitment to tithe and give. Tithing is an act of honouring God (not just an obligation to pay Him first). This along with the act of giving releases more blessing on you than you can imagine.

External to all money matters but of utmost importance, seek after God first and foremost and whatever you need or desire, He will provide.

Educate Yourself about Personal Finance

You're in a good place. This workbook is a resource to educate yourself—biblically and practically. The more you know and understand, the better equipped you are to make sound financial and life decisions.

If you haven't read it already, be sure to pick up a copy of my book Financial Empowerment at https://www.amazon.com/dp/B00AQXMAT0 as this will clarify some of what is being covered in this workbook. Also make sure to read blogs, books and take courses that would help you in becoming a better money manager.

Get Help from Financial Professionals

Beyond reading and participating in courses on personal finance, you might need to consider acquiring the assistance of a financial professional. You might need financial professionals such as your banker, a debt counsellor, an insurance agent or an investment advisor depending on the area you need assistance in. With respect to overall money management, a financial planner or a money coach can assist you in reaching your financial goals.

Don't Get Too Comfortable With Money

Money is a tool to use for your benefit and for others as well. Therefore, don't love it or fear it; rather, manage it. Take the emotion out of money by managing it objectively. How? Constantly remind yourself that it isn't yours in the first place even though you are fully responsible for it now. The reality is that you have to give God a report on how you've managed not only money, but how you've lived the gift of life He gave to you.

Automate, Automate, and Automate

Wherever possible, automate transactions that occur on a regular basis—savings, tithing and giving, mortgage payment or rent, bill payments, credit card payment, vehicle loan or other loan repayments. This reduces the mental, physical and emotional effort required to do these activities and eliminates unnecessary stress and cost associated with missing bill or loan payments or making savings and investments.

Ask God to Help You Be a Good Manager

Whatever you do in life, it takes the grace of God to succeed or thrive. If you think you're bad at this money management thing, ask God to make you good at it. If you think you are a fairly good money manager, ask Him to make you a better one.

Make a Personal Commitment

Every change starts with a thought or a decision. Today, decide. Are you going to let money rule or overtake your life, or are you going to rule and manage it and let it serve you instead? Make a commitment today to change your relationship with money and become the master over it.

One important aspect of this commitment is to understand WHY you are doing this. Maybe you want a less stressed life, financial freedom, a new house, a higher education for your child, to be able afford or maintain the current lifestyle you have, or to have a strong financial future. Whatever your reason, DO what is necessary to make it happen and constantly ask God for the Financial

Grace to be the best money manager He is pleased with.

Now it is time to get to the work of managing your money more effectively.

ORGANIZE YOUR FINANCES: NECESSARY FOR YOUR SUCCESS

By faith [that is, with an inherent trust and enduring confidence in the power, wisdom and goodness of God] we understand that the worlds (universe, ages) were framed and created [formed, put in order, and equipped for their intended purpose] *by the word of God, so that what is seen was not made out of things which are visible.* — Hebrews 11:3 (AMP)

You may be wondering: "What does that scripture verse have to do with my personal finances?" My response to you is: "A whole lot!" Here's what I received as I meditated on this word. It takes work to get your life looking like what you want it to be, but it starts with putting things in order.

When you read Genesis 1, you see God at work. He took a void, disorderly earth and created and brought into order the beautiful and amazing universe we experience today. Before the earth and the universe could function as it does today—day and night, summer, spring, winter, fall, cycles of growth and multiplication and a whole lot more—God had to bring it into order.

Before you can experience financial success or financial empowerment, you have to set your financial life in order. Just as God ordered or formed the earth and the heavens, you and I can form or bring order to our financial lives.

At the beginning of this workbook, you started this financial empowerment journey by addressing and resetting your thoughts and feelings towards God and money. Those exercises were a necessary part of putting your financial life in order. You have and will continue to reshape your thought life to reflect God's will for you and your finances. Now to cement those new beginnings, you will do the work of organizing your finances.

Order leads to success and being organized is a continuous process necessary for living financially empowered. Right now, you may be operating from a position of disorder in your finances or other areas of your life. There might be some clutter or a sense of chaos. You may might not have your important personal and financial information properly filed, or you may not know what your financial position is.

Life can be busy to say the least, and I know you might think that you don't have time for this. However, think of it this way: it's less stressful (especially when faced with life's challenges such as a family emergency or health issues) to know where your important information is located. It is easier to locate if stored in one place and also if that is known by your loved ones. It is a good practice to bring and to keep your paperwork well-organized.

Do You Have Your Life in Order?

How organized are you financially? Being financially organized is often seen as a drudgery or as an activity that would take the life out of living. Below are a few questions to find out how much you need to get yourself organized. If you can answer these questions with a strong 'Yes' then you can relax. If your response is 'No' to any of these, then you have some work to do.

Question	Yes or No?
Can you easily find all of your important financial documents (e.g. insurance policies, mortgage papers, lease agreements, account opening documents, proof of ownership)?	
Are these documents accessible to family members (a select few) in case they are urgently needed when you are not available?	
What about non-financial documents (e.g. birth certificate, passports, citizenship information, marriage certificate, etc.), do you have them sorted and filed in one place?	
Do you have a written will or living trust? Do you know where this document is kept?	
Do you know how much money you owe to others?	
Do you know the value of what you own?	

I'm sure that there may be a few 'No's' in response to the above, but that's okay. You are on the road to financial empowerment. You are here to get things going in the right direction and in alignment to God's will. Don't you worry about the 'No's'. You will tackle them one at a time.

A Few Tips to Keep You Organized

Here are a few tips on how you can become financially organized and continue to keep clutter out of your finances.

- Know where your important documents are
- Develop a filing system – hard copy and e-copy
- Make good use of your computer to keep record of your money activities
- Have a drop box – a central place for your mail until you can review it
- Remove the clutter from your wallet regularly
- Involve your family to keep things in order

The exercises that follow are designed to help you get a good start on organizing yourself. You don't have to do exactly as I have suggested. Hopefully, you will get some ideas on how you can better organize your finances. Ask yourself the question: What can I do to make the money management process easier for me and my family? Based on your lifestyle and activity, I am sure that you can come up with the best way for you. Be sure to seek help anytime you feel overwhelmed. Don't let clutter stress you. Be organized.

Tools Needed to Get Organized

You will need the following items:

- ☐ One three-ring binder for each family member
- ☐ A pack of sheet protectors (8.5" x 11" or other document size). These are available in packages of 25s, 50s or 100s. Estimate how much you need to start with depending on the size of your family.
- ☐ Alternatively, a folder with 12 slots or more would also work
- ☐ A few extra-large envelopes for oversized documents that you don't want to fold. You will need to note on the front what these contain and place them in the back of the binder
- ☐ A marker or pen or your computer and printer
- ☐ A pack of file folders and file labels and/or a 12-month folder wallet

COLLECT ALL YOUR PERMANENT DOCUMENTS
- ☐ **Permanent documents** include any financial, legal or other documents that are valid for more than one year.
  - o Financial Permanent Documents include: a will or living trust, insurance policies (life, health, business related, etc.), mortgage agreement, title deed, loan agreements, all account opening documents for bank accounts, lines of credit, and investment or brokerage accounts and share certificates.

- o Non-financial Permanent documents: birth and/or baptism certificates, immunization records, educational certificates, passports or other documents regarding proof of nationality or citizenship.
  - o I haven't listed all the documents, but this is a start. Give this some thought and add to the list. Make sure that your spouse, the Executor of your will and other responsible family member know where these documents are kept and how to access them.
- ☐ Place each document in a sheet protector and file in the folder in alphabetical order. As mentioned earlier, have a binder for each family member. This makes for easier retrieval of information.
- ☐ Create a written or typed list of all documents included and insert it at the front of the folder or binder so you can easily and quickly find out what is inside.

GATHER ALL YOUR TEMPORARY DOCUMENTS

- ☐ Whereas permanent documents are long-term, temporary documents are those which are valid for a year or less.
  - o **Temporary documents include** regular monthly bills, bank statements, loan payment receipts, vehicle insurance policies that are renewable annually, short-term purchase or lease agreements.
- ☐ To file these types of documents, you can consider one of these options:
- ☐ File by name alphabetically for every organisation or person that you conduct business with. Filing by name, especially for bank and investment accounts, car loans, mortgage and other organizations for which you may have related permanent documents, is best for easy access of this type of information.
- ☐ File by month, in which case all the bills and receipts for the month are kept in one folder or file slot. For this method, you can use a file wallet with 12 slots – one for each month. Filing by month can be easy since you just have to drop the paper in the slot related to the month. The drawback with this option is when you need to find all the receipts or invoices related to a particular vendor or organization; you will have to go into each month's slot.

FinEmp Power Tip: Get Help

At the initial stages to avoid being overwhelmed with getting organized, you will need help. Involve the family (including your children) in this process for two reasons:

1. It takes the load off you to do it alone. As the Word says, a three-strung cord is not easily

broken. And as another saying goes, more hands make light work.

2. It's a good way of sharing with them what you are doing and relieves the pressure off you if they are know where important documents are being kept.

ACTION STEP EXTRA: KEEPING ORGANIZED ELECTRONICALLY

In this electronic age, there is a necessity to keep certain details at your fingertips. For myself, I have created a **password-protected spreadsheet** which I maintain on a consistent basis with any information that can be easily recorded electronically for quick access. This eliminates the need to refer to the physical document each time.

Document types	Information recorded
Online credentials for websites	url, username, password
Financial / Bank account information	card numbers, account name, online access username and password, insurance policy numbers, contact details for all institutions dealt with
Contact information for anyone	friends, family, co-workers, business connections, etc., are kept on my phone and google contacts as a backup
Educational details	institution, location, grade and date of achievement
Employment history	employer name, address, telephone no., start date and end date of employment, position titles, promotions, achievements (most of this should be in a resume, but you can also keep track of other work-related information you consider useful to your career growth)
Personal details	passport numbers, driver's license numbers, other identification numbers and the associated expiry dates for each, etc.
Business related information	incorporation or business registration details, banking information, documents of administrative, marketing, etc. (note: apart from keeping this on your computer consider having a backup system e.g. an external drive, cloud backup service)

Note: This activity is not required, but if you see the need you can do this another time.

FINANCIALLY SPEAKING, HOW ARE YOU DOING TODAY?

Take care to know the condition of your flocks, and pay attention to your herds. For wealth doesn't last forever, neither does a crown through all generations. — Proverbs 27:23-24 (CJB)

Please don't cringe. If you've come this far, you are making great progress and you can move ahead strong. Don't worry, this is just one out of many times to come that you will need to do this in order to become and remain financially empowered. But each time it will become easier to do.

Just as it is necessary to review the financial position or condition of a business, so it is with your personal life. Yes, the responsibility of managing your finances is like that of running a business. You need to know where you are at (your financial position) in order to determine what you need to do to get from there to your desired result (your new and improved financial positions and conditions).

Here's how you will review your finances. First from a non-numbers perspective, you will answer a few questions. Here you want to get a 'feel' of how you see your financial life before digging into specific figures. The reality is: you know where you are at mentally even before you do any figure churning. Then from a numbers view, you will do a simple calculation to see where you're at financially. Once you have your financial position clarified you can work through each area of your finances to make some necessary improvements.

Circle of Financial Perspective

In the diagram below—the circle of Financial Perspective—first rate yourself in each of the following financial life areas: earning (or wealth creation), tithing, saving and investing, spending, giving and lending, borrowing, (financial) planning.

- ☐ **Where do you find yourself today, financially?** On a scale of 1 to 10, with 10 being the most satisfied, write the number inside each area.
- ☐ Next, rate yourself in each of these areas in the future. **Where would you like to be at the end of this year? What is your money dream improvement mark?** Write that rating outside each area.

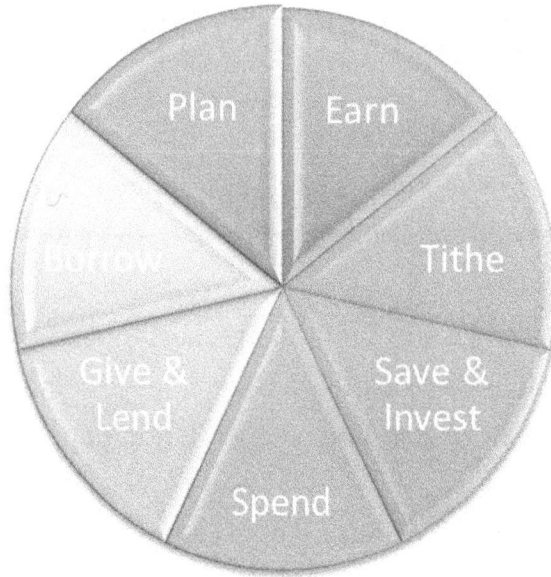

Now that you've done that, there are a few questions to help you clarify why you selected the rating above. Most of these questions require a 'Yes' or 'No' response, but where applicable add a comment or figure if you know it.

	Yes / No	Comments
Are you happy with your current income level?		
Do you pay a tithe (10% of your gross income) to God?		
Have you saved any money in the past 12 months?		
Would you say that your spending is excessive?		
Do you know your current financial position (how much you own less how much you owe)?		
Do you have a financial plan?		

Looking back, what would you have done differently in your finances?

_____

_____

_____

_____

_____

_____

_____

_____

_____

_____

What areas of your finances is the Lord leading you to align to His will?

_____

_____

_____

_____

_____

_____

_____

_____

_____

_____

_____

_____

_____

What areas do you think you need to improve or focus on going forward?

_____

_____

_____

_____

_____

_____

_____

_____

_____

_____

_____

_____

_____

Well done! Now what you've done the heart work, it is time to churn some numbers.

My Financial Position

Your financial position is a summary picture of what you have and what you owe to others at a specific date. The net figure of your assets less your liabilities is called your Net Worth. Before you start choose the date – it is best to work with the last day of a month e.g. 31 December, 2018. Then gather up the balances for each of the items listed below and enter them into the worksheet.

DESCRIPTION	Amount	Account #	Other Details
ASSETS			
Long term assets:			
Real Estate			
Vehicle			
Other long-term asset			
Investments:			
Golden Years Savings			
Brokerage Account #1			
Brokerage Account #2			
Other Investments			
Other Assets:			
Jewellery			
Personal Effects			
Household Items (furniture, appliances)			
Liquid Accounts:			
Checking Account			
Emergency Fund – Freedom Fund			
Special Savings – Specific Goal			

DESCRIPTION	Amount	Account #	Other Details
Money Market			
TOTAL ASSETS			
LIABILITIES			
Long-term debt:			
Mortgage			
Car Loan			
Student Loan			
Other Loans			
Short-term debt:			
Credit Card #1			
Credit Card #2			
Line of Credit or Other debt			
TOTAL LIABILITIES			
NET WORTH			

CREATE WEALTH: WITH GOD'S ANOINTING

But you shall remember [with profound respect] the Lord your God, for it is He who is giving you power to make wealth, that He may confirm His covenant which He swore (solemnly promised) to your fathers, as it is this day. — Deuteronomy 8:17-18 (AMP)

Every time I read this, I am reminded that whatever wealth I had, have and will have is all because of God's anointing on my life. I am thankful for the strength He gives me to work. What about you? Are you thankful for the ability God gives you to work? Or do you not like your work?

In this section, the main purpose is to understand what you think or feel about your work. You will determine if your work is satisfying, what you like, and what you would like to change. You will also take a deep look at yourself and what God has placed in you. Then you will review your current income level before moving on to how you use it.

Roadblocks to Creating Wealth

Wealth. This word is like a taboo in Christian circles, but yet God talks about wealth and He even describes what a wealthy person is like. See Deuteronomy 8:12-13, *... when you have eaten and are full, and have built beautiful houses and dwell in them; and when your herds and your flocks multiply, and your silver and your gold are multiplied, and all that you have is multiplied.*

Do you need to eat? Wouldn't you like a beautiful house to live in? And yes, it would be nice if your work, your money and everything you have increase, right? This is as much as I would say on this word. My next question then is, do you have an issue with creating wealth?

Read the following statements about wealth and check any that apply to you.

- ☐ I don't believe that God is interested in my work or my money.
- ☐ I don't see the need to involve God in my finances or in my daily work activity.
- ☐ I have what I have because I am able, capable, educated and connected to the right people.
- ☐ This wealth thing isn't for me. Too much money is sinful or will lead to sin.
- ☐ I don't believe God wants me to be wealthy or have more than enough. I've been

struggling financially for a long time.

☐ I don't have the education or skill to make the kind of money I want to earn.

☐ There's no point being creative or thinking big, I can't do anything about it anyways. I'd rather be level-headed and practical than go off trying and failing.

☐ I just don't have it in me anymore—the drive to keep going to make anything extra. I leave that for someone else to do.

Did you identify with any of these statements? If yes, then ask God to rewrite your mental framework about creating wealth to be aligned to His will for you. God wants you to create wealth!

Is Your Work Fulfilling?

God gives you the power to create wealth. He gives you the anointing to do what you are good at. He gives you the ability to shine at the skill, talent, knowledge or expertise that He has placed in you. One thing I have noticed is that for many, life happens and we often settle for doing what is necessary rather than what is fulfilling. If you were to look back at your career or business choices, for the most part you made decisions based on your immediate circumstances. You may have chosen a career path similar to one of your parents because that's what you saw them do or that is what was available at the time. You may have taken a job because it was readily available and you needed the money. Years later you find yourself where you didn't want to be and you may think that you can't make any changes now. Life circumstances can often dictate our decisions and box us into situations we deep down inside long to change.

But there is hope. **God created you to experience fulfilment through work.** So if you aren't fulfilled in doing the daily grind, then it's time for you the assess where you are and create a plan of action to move ahead either into a promotion in your current job, a new career, a self-employed profession or freelance (side-business) or full-time business. Whatever it might be, you can make it happen with God as your Help and Guide.

How can you know if you're happy at work? Check the statement(s) which apply to you:

☐ I don't enjoy my job. I dread going to work every day.

☐ Work feels like a curse. It's too stressful most of the time.

☐ I am just doing this job to provide for myself and my family but I don't like it

☐ I think I should be enjoying life, not working all the time

☐ I work but I don't make enough money. It's a struggle most of the time.

Did anything above resonate with you? If so, then go to next section entitled **What Do You Have?** If not and you are happy in your work, feel free to keep the next few sections and move on to **Is Your Current Income Level Enough?**.

WHAT DO YOU HAVE?

Here are some tough questions. This deals with you—your strengths, interests, skills, knowledge. It's time to take a pause and learn what God has placed in you that you can use to benefit you, not only financially but intellectually, emotionally, physically and even spiritually. This requires you to take a pause from the busyness of life, get alone with yourself and God, and assess the special you that you are.

What are your top five **STRENGTHS** (your personality traits and attitudes)?

_____

_____

_____

_____

_____

_____

_____

What are your **INTERESTS** or what are you most **PASSIONATE about** (i.e. what problem do you wish to see solved, what do you talk about a lot, what do you enjoy so much that you get lost in it? (Hint: this is often the key to knowing God's purpose for you.)

_____

_____

_____

_____

_____

_____

_____

What are your top five **SKILLS** (i.e. what do you do well)?

_____

_____

_____

_____

_____

_____

_____

What **KNOWLEDGE** or **EXPERTISE** do you have (e.g. educational background, life-changing experience, wisdom)?

_____

_____

_____

_____

_____

_____

_____

What do others say you are very gifted at or that you do so well?

_____

_____

_____

_____

_____

_____

_____

What changes would you have to make to fulfil your purpose while improving your current income level?

_____

_____

_____

_____

_____

_____

_____

Cheers! I applaud you for completing this exercise. Well done! (However, if you haven't done it, go back up and start working on it.) This exercise will go a long way as you work through the upcoming sessions of the workbook. It's hard work, I know, but it is well worth it.

You will realize that you need to make changes in your life, whether it is for the purpose of increasing your income level or in order to start doing fulfilling work that aligns with God's purpose for your life. Don't allow anything or anyone to hold you back. Don't allow even yourself (hidden or known fears, naysayers, etc.) to stop you from fulling your financial and spiritual destiny.

Also, as you work through this program, consider the positive impact that you can have on others—your family, your community, your church family, friends, co-workers or the world at large. The possibilities are endless. It's time to start making changes and plunge ahead in faith.

Wealth Creation Alternatives – Multiple Streams of Income

Here is a list of freelance projects, skills and trades to help you get started on recognizing your next career, side-gig or new business. These ideas are just a starting list of special skills, tasks and activities that you can use to get inspired. Check the ones that the interest you and line up with your previous responses.

- ☐ Accounting and bookkeeping
- ☐ Acquire parts from electronic stores
- ☐ Affiliate sales and marketing
- ☐ Antique refurbishment
- ☐ Art collector
- ☐ Audio production
- ☐ Automobile / Motorcycle repair
- ☐ Baby sitter
- ☐ Baker (specialty)
- ☐ Blogging / blog consulting
- ☐ Build a niche website
- ☐ Business consulting
- ☐ Business training
- ☐ Business writing (business plans, grants, proposals)
- ☐ Buy and sell domain names
- ☐ Buy used electronics and refurbish them
- ☐ Car washing and detailing
- ☐ Care giving
- ☐ Career counselling or coaching

- ☐ Lead generation
- ☐ Licensed product distributor
- ☐ Life coaching (career, business, spiritual, financial, wellness, etc.)
- ☐ Make custom furniture
- ☐ Make handmade jewellery
- ☐ Making decorations (seasonal with local material)
- ☐ Marketing / technology
- ☐ Martial arts instruction
- ☐ Mobile laundry service
- ☐ Modelling
- ☐ Music instructor
- ☐ Newsletter or magazine publishing
- ☐ Online coaching
- ☐ Online courses
- ☐ Online news correspondent
- ☐ Online sales (Amazon, Esty, Ebay)
- ☐ Online subcontracting
- ☐ Patent something
- ☐ Pay-per-click advertising (PPC)

- ☐ Career help (finding work, optimizing resumes, cover letters, interviews)
- ☐ Carpet cleaning
- ☐ Catering business
- ☐ Child care
- ☐ Clothing alternations and tailoring
- ☐ Coaching sports teams
- ☐ Commission only sales
- ☐ Community management / promotion
- ☐ Computer networking
- ☐ Computer repair
- ☐ Computer training and lessons
- ☐ Contract consumer service
- ☐ Cooking / personal chef
- ☐ Copywriting and editing
- ☐ Courier services
- ☐ Daily money manager service
- ☐ Dance / choreography
- ☐ Dance instructor
- ☐ Data analysis
- ☐ Database administration
- ☐ Dating / social skills
- ☐ Delivery service
- ☐ Design (brochures, business cards, logos)
- ☐ Develop an app
- ☐ Dog walking
- ☐ EBooks
- ☐ E-commerce consulting
- ☐ Education (College prep, Math, English)
- ☐ Event planning / promotion
- ☐ Fashion / image consulting
- ☐ Fill out online surveys
- ☐ Fiverr gigs
- ☐ Freelance content marketing

- ☐ Personal assistant
- ☐ Personal chef
- ☐ Personal fitness trainer
- ☐ Pet services (grooming, walking, etc.)
- ☐ Pet sitter
- ☐ Phone case business
- ☐ Photography
- ☐ Physical therapy
- ☐ Pool cleaning
- ☐ Portrait photographer
- ☐ Presentation design consultant
- ☐ Productivity coaching
- ☐ Programming / web development
- ☐ Project management
- ☐ Property manager
- ☐ Public relations
- ☐ Public speaking
- ☐ Public speaking outreach
- ☐ Real estate appraiser
- ☐ Real estate sales consultant
- ☐ Remote English teacher/tutor
- ☐ Rent your car
- ☐ Research
- ☐ Sales
- ☐ Search engine optimization (SEO)
- ☐ Selling handmade clothing and garments
- ☐ Small business marketing
- ☐ Sports / Personal Training
- ☐ Stock photographer
- ☐ Strategic / management consulting
- ☐ Task rabbit (i.e. Do odd jobs)
- ☐ Tax and financial planning
- ☐ Tax preparation (individual and corporate)

- ☐ Freelance eBook writing
- ☐ Freelance proofreading and editing
- ☐ General computer help / training
- ☐ Ghost writer
- ☐ Google Analytics
- ☐ Google paid ad specialist
- ☐ Graphic design
- ☐ Home maintenance / organizing
- ☐ House cleaning
- ☐ House sitter
- ☐ Human resources / payroll services
- ☐ Instagram marketing
- ☐ Interior design consultant
- ☐ Internet marketing consulting
- ☐ Invest other people's money (i.e. trader)
- ☐ Invest your money
- ☐ IT Security
- ☐ Junk removal service
- ☐ Justice of peace (or public notary)
- ☐ Landing page specialist
- ☐ Lawn mowing
- ☐ Technical writing
- ☐ Tile cleaning and grouting
- ☐ Tour guide
- ☐ Transcription / scoping services
- ☐ Translator
- ☐ Travel consultant
- ☐ Travel Planning
- ☐ Tutor for specific subjects and grade levels
- ☐ Tutoring and coaching
- ☐ User interface & user experience (UI/UX)
- ☐ Vehicle advertising
- ☐ Video production / editing
- ☐ Virtual assistant
- ☐ Web design
- ☐ Wedding photographer
- ☐ Wedding planner
- ☐ Window cleaning services
- ☐ WordPress website consultant
- ☐ Writer (fiction or non-fiction)
- ☐ Writing greeting cards
- ☐ Yard work or gardening services

How Do You Move Ahead?

Now that you have learned what you have in YOU, it's time to choose 1 to 3 interests that you would like to pursue. If you have at least one area you're really interested in pursuing, that's enough to get started. However, if you choose more than one, you can always come back and start with your next choice if your first choice doesn't work out!

Look at what you previously did (strengths, interests, etc.). Are there any similarities or common traits? List at least three income generating options you can consider building on in the future.

_____

_____

_____

Also, ask yourself the following to gain further clarity:

Is this a full-time opportunity or a side-gig that can complement your current income?

_____

_____

_____

_____

_____

_____

_____

Do you want to do this online or locally?

_____

_____

_____

_____

_____

_____

_____

_____

Is this a potentially profitable venture?

_____

_____

_____

_____

_____

_____

_____

Is it affordable, i.e. can you start with a small amount of money or will you need more capital?

_____

_____

_____

_____

_____

_____

Can you enlist family, friends or knowledgeable people in the industry to help you?

_____

_____

_____

_____

_____

_____

_____

Brainstorm Your Income Generation Idea

I thought it prudent to leave this space for you to explore your ideas some more. You may be full of many thoughts right now and ideas might be flowing freely and quickly. Don't miss the opportunity to get it down on paper. When you write it, it not only frees your mind, but it becomes etched in your mind what you want to achieve. The vision becomes clearer. So go ahead, make your vision clear to you!

_____

_____

_____

_____

_____

_____

_____

_____

_____

_____

_____

_____

_____

_____

_____

_____

_____
_____
_____
_____
_____
_____
_____
_____
_____
_____
_____
_____
_____
_____
_____
_____
_____
_____
_____
_____
_____
_____
_____

If you need help in developing a plan to move ahead, you can check the following resources. It would be my pleasure to serve you: I offer professional writing services and career coaching, if you are looking to make career changes. Also as a life coach, I can work with you to guide you through goal setting and goal achievement. Go to http://www.pamelavcarmichael.com/living-success-shop.

Is Your Current Income Level Enough?

I am sure you said an outright "Of course, not. I need more money." With that thought, you probably started thinking about the cost of living increases that you've had within the past year and the fact that there hasn't been any equivalent increase in your salary or business income to match. I get you. I understand where you are coming from.

But the question still remains, is your current income level enough? Considering your lifestyle, your family structure, where you live, your day-to-day expenses, future goals and personal values, do you think you should be able to comfortably live on the income you currently receive or do you really need an increase? If so, by how much?

When you work, create something, offer a service, you are not just working to get paid. You are giving of what the Creator God has placed in you—knowledge, understanding, experience, skill, energy—you are working out your potential. To charge for what you do isn't against the laws of God. After all, the Apostle Paul tells us clearly that if you don't work then you shouldn't eat. People are actually honoring you and God when they pay you for what you do. Jesus also said that a worker is worthy of his hire or to be paid.

How much do you currently earn? Write it down:

My Current Income	Amount*	Annual Amount
Gross income		
Income taxes		
Social insurance		
Net income		
Pension plan		
Health plan		
Other deductions		
Net Disposable income		
Average other living expenses		
Net Cash flow		

*The amount entered here is based on the frequency with which you receive income: weekly, bi-monthly or monthly. You may already know these figures, but it helps to write them out to have a clear vision of what you receive. Sometimes people are shocked at what passes through their hands or bank accounts on an annual basis.

What do you think, do you earn enough? No need to answer this question right now. The next five sessions will cover what you do with what you receive. After we have some actual figures to work with and you have made some adjustments, you may consider this income good or you may conclude that you do need more. Let us forge ahead so you can become financially empowered and have more than enough to be a blessing to others.

TITHE: HONOUR GOD FIRST

They said, "[The Emperor Tiberius] Caesar's." Then He said to them, "Then pay to Caesar the things that are Caesar's; and to God the things that are God's." — Matthew 22:21 (AMP)

"Challenge God to bless you when you tithe. He'll do it!" — Pamela Carmichael

It has been debated for many years about whether tithing is Biblical and/or if it is a New Testament practice. Frankly, New Testament believers give way beyond the tithe (Act 4:32-37). In any case, I have no hesitation in encouraging you to tithe to God. I have been tithing since I first gave my life to Christ in my teens and have experienced no disadvantage in doing so. I have only seen God's faithfulness—even in challenging economic times, He always provides. I hope that you tithe and experience the same.

If however you have issues with tithing, list your reasons here. After you've done that list, take a pause and ask the Lord Jesus to help you overcome any mental or emotional blocks regarding the tithe. Seek Him for an openness so that you can understand His will for you concerning tithing and becoming an effective manager of the financial and other resources He has given to you.

Understanding the Blessing of Tithing

In my book – *Financial Empowerment: Realign Your Finances to God's Will* I discussed some of the benefits, blessings and perspectives you might have concerning tithing. For each of these I provided supporting Biblical truths for study. If you haven't read the book and want to read this section on tithing, you can get a copy here: https://www.amazon.com/dp/B00AQXMAT0.

In this section of the workbook I want you to study the word of God as it relates to the practice of tithing. While you are doing this, ask the Holy Spirit to clarify any questions, doubts, concerns about tithing. Then move forward.

Below I have provided a summary of what the tithe is or does in your life. In some cases I have indicated supporting Bible verses for the blessings and benefits of tithing. This is not by any means an exhaustive list. Feel free to add to the list and to include additional supporting scriptures that speak to you as the Holy Spirit guides you.

The tithe ...	Bible verses
1. Seals the covenant between you and God	*And Abram gave him a tenth of all* [the treasure he had taken in battle]. - Gen. 14:20 (AMP) *Then Jacob made a vow (promise), saying, "If God will be with me and will keep me on this journey that I take, and will give me food to eat and clothing to wear, and if* [He grants that] *I return to my father's house in safety, then the Lord will be my God. This stone which I have set up as a pillar (monument, memorial) will be God's house* [a sacred place to me], *and of everything that You give me I will give the tenth to You* [as an offering to signify my gratitude and dependence on You]." - Gen. 28: 20-22 (AMP)
2. Is holy to the Lord	*And all the tithe (tenth part) of the land, whether the seed of the land or the fruit of the tree, is the Lord's; it is holy to the Lord.* - Leviticus 27:30 (AMP)
3. Blesses you and protects you	Malachi 3:10-11
4. Keeps the spirit of mammon from controlling you	Matthew 6:24
5. Is a seek-you-first the kingdom of God practice	Matthew 6:33
6. Is giving back to God what is rightfully His	Malachi 3:8-9 *"Caesar's,"* they replied. Jesus said, *"Precisely, for the coin bears the image of the emperor Caesar. Well, then, you should pay the emperor what is due to the emperor. But because you bear the image of God, give back to God all that belongs to him."* — Matthew 22:21 (TPT)

7. Keeps you from being selfish, you care for others. This also destroys the spirit of consumerism and hoarding.	*"When you have finished laying aside all the tithe of your increase in the third year—the year of tithing—and have given it to the Levite, the stranger, the fatherless, and the widow, so that they may eat within your gates and be filled,..."* — Deut. 26:12-16
8. Is an act of worship or honor to God	*If you don't tithe you rob God and therefore dishonor Him.* Malachi 3: 8-9
9. Is a way to keep life in perspective; reminding you that God is your Source	Malachi 3:10
10. Is a destroyer that stops the attacks of the enemy in your life	Malachi 3:11
11. Is a means through which you become a blessing	Malachi 3:10,12
12. Beautifies you	Malachi 3: 12
13. Is an act of obedience to God's command	Malachi 3:9
14. Is a poverty breaker. Instead of having less you have more.	Malachi 3:11 Prov. 3:9-10

Take Action: Tithe

I hope that what you have read and worked through so far has removed any hesitation you may have about tithing. When God—who gave it all and owns it all—says to you to bring some back to His storehouse, how can you in your heart say no? My friend, Trust God and tithe. If God has instructed it then do it. Since God has promised a blessing to those who tithe, then believe and expect that He will follow through on His promises (Malachi 3:10-12).

So that you are clear on what amount you have to tithe on a weekly, bi-monthly or monthly basis, take time out to calculate what your tithe should be.

How Much is My Tithe?

Again, this can be debatable if we let it. But I would rather put it this way, if the government takes taxes from you based on your gross income (and they are clearly limited in their ability to help you), then your tithe to God should be based on your gross income (the One who is the Source of all good things you receive). From that perspective, it is clear isn't it? Therefore your tithe is 10% of your gross income.

	Example of Tithing Calculation	**My Tithe is**
Gross income	(per month) $5,000	
Tithe (10%) – Due to God	$500	

Right now, stop here. Take your check book and write the tithe to your local church. Alternatively, go online or visit your bank and setup a direct debit transaction to have the tithe sent to your local church on a consistent basis. As you do this you will feel relief and peace. God Bless you.

However, don't stop there. Oftentimes we receive monetary gifts or have additional income streams. We may even receive interest payments or dividends on investments or another form of income that was expected or unexpected. These too are blessings from the Lord and we ought to tithe on any increase we receive.

Make it a habit that every time you receive money immediately make a mental calculation how much is due to the Lord. As soon as possible, write that check or withdraw the amount and place it in an offering envelope. Place it in your Bible or whatever you take to church so you don't forget it. Better yet, if you can transfer the amount to your church's account then by all means do so.

Let tithing be your first priority to God every time you receive financially.

A Prayer on Tithing

If you are already a faithful tither, yet you don't see the blessings God has promised, then consider this: do you believe God's word? Tithing requires faith—faith that God will honour His word to pour out blessings on you as well as to keep the devourer from destroying the work of your hands.

Take a few minutes to pray for God's grace to obey His word concerning tithing.

> Lord, thank you for being my Faithful God and Father. You are my Ultimate Source! You are my Provider!

> Lord, your will be done in me! Help me to honour you by obeying you. Help me to always bring my tithes and offerings into your storehouse. Let your will be done in my local church and help the leadership to use the tithes and offerings received to further the gospel in various ways as you deem it fit.

> Provide for me each day what I need for the now and the future. Provide in ways beyond my imagination and more than I need so I can bless others too.

> Father, forgive me for those times I have chosen not to tithe. Even so, forgive me for not trusting in your ability to take care of me. Help me not to yield to any financial temptations that will dishonour you in anyway.

> Keep me from evil. Bless the work of my hands and bring increase to my finances as I return the tithe to you.

> Let your kingdom come and your will be done in every area of my life. All honour and glory to you forever! Let it be done, in Jesus' Name.

My Tithing Commitment

Take a few moments to complete this commitment form. If needed, post it where you can see it often (e.g. in your Bible or on your desk). This is a commitment you are making to God, but also to yourself. You will always benefit from paying the tithe.

My Tithing Commitment

I, _____ make a commitment to God and myself
to faithfully tithe on every increase I receive.

- ☐ **I will start tithing**
- ☐ **I will continue to tithe**
- ☐ **I will start giving above the tithe**
- ☐ **I will continue giving above the tithe**
- ☐ **I will tithe or will continue to tithe on a regular basis (weekly / monthly)**

Based on my gross income, I estimate that my tithe will be $_____
(per week / per month).

I believe that God will provide more than enough for me and my family. I will also
be a blessing to others. Because of my tithe, God will keep my work from being
destroyed. All those who know me will call me blessed!

Signature: _____ Date: _____

*"Bring the whole tithe into the storehouse, that there may be food in my house. Test
me in this," says the Lord Almighty, "and see if I will not throw open the floodgates of
heaven and pour out so much blessing that there will not be room enough to store it."*
– Malachi 3:10

SAVE: PAY YOURSELF TOO

"The plan to make money but not save some of it is incomplete." — Pamela Carmichael

The 'spending' habit must be replaced by the 'saving habit' by all who attain financial independence.
— Napoleon Hill, *The Laws of Success*

Why Aren't You Saving Money?

Who do you work for? Is it for you to pay bills and have nothing left to enjoy now and in your latter years? Or do you work to provide for yourself and family and help others in your community (church and beyond)? Most of us work and see the money only for a short while in our bank accounts. We pay others before we pay ourselves (government included) and then we tell ourselves that we don't work for enough money. Although in some cases that may be true, the reality is that most of the time we don't consider giving ourselves a paycheck.

What are your reasons for not saving? Check any of the comments that apply to you and later on we will address how to overcome these challenges:

- I like to have nice things. I don't see why I should work so hard and not be rewarded
- Honestly, my income isn't enough. By the time I pay everything I should, there isn't much left over
- I spend more than earned. No matter what I do I have to use the credit cards to cover monthly living expenses
- I have more debt than I have savings. Frankly, there isn't anything left to save
- My mortgage payments are too high. I wish I had bought a smaller house
- I operate on a one-income stream household and it just isn't enough for my family
- I don't see the point of saving anything. You don't even get a decent interest rate these days.
- As soon as I set aside some money something happens and I have to spend it
- I don't want to get caught up with earthly things and be like the Rich Fool

What other reasons can you think of for not being able to save on a regular basis?

_____

_____

_____

_____

_____

_____

_____

Reasons to Save Money

If you want to be financially empowered, free from swarming debt and build a positive future for you and your family, you will need to develop the habit of saving. Although this list is covered in my book – *Financial Empowerment: Realign Your Finances to God's Will* (https://www.amazon.com/dp/B00AQXMAT0) let me outline a few reasons why it is important to save money on a consistent basis. You should save money:

- ✓ To give yourself your own paycheck. – Not all your money should go to creditors. Boost your own economy.
- ✓ To help kick the habit of spending. – Making saving the second money step in your Financial Empowerment process will help curb the habit of spending. How is that? The money you save shouldn't be readily available for use – out of sight is often out of mind. The less money you see in your checking account to spend, the less you will spend.
- ✓ For you and your family's future. – This should always be in the forefront of your mind: The people you are working for are waiting for you at home. Your money isn't only for the present—to provide food, clothing and shelter—but to have for the future needs of your household.
- ✓ To avoid the stress of not having when unexpected emergencies happen. – Life happens and in this fallen world there are curve balls and setbacks to deal with. Most of the time they require some kind of financial outlay. Be prepared by saving for these times.
- ✓ For a good reason. – Give savings a positive assignment. For example, save money for the downpayment on a house and for the initial expenses of owning a property.
- ✓ To be ready for new opportunities. – Having assets like savings makes it easier for financial institutions to lend to you if you need funds for a good investment. Why? They see you as being financially sound if you are a consistent saver and someone with low debt. PEOPLE WHO HAVE MONEY HAVE OPPORTUNITY. You cannot invest if you don't have what it takes (i.e. money)

The Biblical View of Saving

Yes, of course the Bible talks about saving. In reading the Old Testament there is much talk about storehouses. In the New Testament, saving does appear to be clearly discussed, but it's encouraged too. Here are a few scriptures to study.

God blesses your savings too!	Deuteronomy 28:8 *The Lord will command the blessing on you in your storehouses and in all to which you set your hand, and He will bless you in the land which the Lord your God is giving you.*
God has storehouses for the abundance He has created and releases what is needed when it's needed.	• The Wind – Psalms 13:5-7 Jeremiah 10:12-13 & 51:15-16 • Snow and hail – Job 38:22 • The Waters (the deep) - Ps. 33: 5-9 • The Rain (in the heavens) – Deut. 28:12 Deuteronomy 28:12 *The Lord will open to you His good treasure, the heavens, to give the rain to your land in its season, and to bless all the work of your hand. You shall lend to many nations, but you shall not borrow.*
The House of the Lord (i.e. the church) is also a storehouse. The purpose of this storehouse was to take care of the needs of the poor, widowed, orphaned and the ministers in the house of the Lord.	Malachi 3:10 - *Bring all the tithes into the storehouse, That there may be food in My house, And try Me now in this," Says the Lord of hosts, "If I will not open for you the windows of heaven And pour out for you such blessing That there will not be room enough to receive it.* Nehemiah 10:38 - *And the priest, the descendant of Aaron, shall be with the Levites when the Levites receive tithes; and the Levites shall bring up a tenth of the tithes to the house of our God, to the rooms of the storehouse.*

	Nehemiah 12:44 – *And at the same time some were appointed over the rooms of the storehouse for the offerings, the firstfruits, and the tithes, to gather into them from the fields of the cities the portions specified by the Law for the priests and Levites; for Judah rejoiced over the priests and Levites who ministered.* Nehemiah 13:12-13 - *Then all Judah brought the tithe of the grain and the new wine and the oil to the storehouse. 13 And I appointed as treasurers over the storehouse Shelemiah the priest and Zadok the scribe, and of the Levites, Pedaiah; and next to them was Hanan the son of Zaccur, the son of Mattaniah; for they were considered faithful, <u>and their task was to distribute to their brethren.</u>*
Your Storehouse – God expects you to save. Instructs you to save.	Genesis 41:56 *He (Joseph) opened the storehouses that housed the extra food that was saved during the times of abundance to sell to others during the times of famine* Deuteronomy 28:8 *God's promise to command the blessing on your savings* Lev. 25:18-22 *The 6th year of blessing was a triple blessing i.e. it was three times the regular harvest or three years of food supply. This meant that the people had to save i.e. store up the excess that was harvested in the 6th year.*

	- The 6th year was the triple blessing year
	- The 7th year was no planting year – use the old supply to feed yourself
	- The 8th year was the planting year – use the old supply to feed yourself
	- The 9th year – use the old supply to feed yourself until the harvesting
Even the ANTS save!	Proverbs 6:6-11 (NLT) *Take a lesson from the ants, you lazybones. Learn from their ways and become wise! Though they have no prince or governor or ruler to make them work, they labor hard all summer, gathering food for the winter. But you, lazybones, how long will you sleep? When will you wake up? A little extra sleep, a little more slumber, a little folding of the hands to rest— then poverty will pounce on you like a bandit; scarcity will attack you like an armed robber.*
The church was instructed to save for the purpose of giving	1 Corinthians 16:2 (AMP) *On the first day of every week each one of you is to put something aside, in proportion to his prosperity, and save it so that no collections* [will need to] *be made when I come.*

How Much Should You Save?
The Financial Empowerment Rule

Most financial advisors will tell you that you should pay yourself first, but as a Christian your first money act is to honour God. After paying your taxes (which are taken out before you see your paycheck) and paying your tithe, you should pay yourself next. You may have heard, read about or even practiced the 50-30-20 rule, or the 70-10-10-10 rule, or some variation of these. You may have adopted the rule of zero-based budgeting where every cent of your money has to be allocated.

However, I want to consider another rule, the **Financial Empowerment Rule** – where the priority and focus of your finances shift from being on yourself and more on your God. Jesus said that the kingdom of God should be your first priority (i.e. have a seek-first mind-set) and everything you need will be given to you by God your Father. As a rule, try to aim for the following:

- ✓ 10% - Tithe
- ✓ 10% - Save
- ✓ 80% - Spend (including personal income taxes)

From my experiences, the saving of 10% hasn't always been perfect. As I've said before, "Life happens." And I have had to delve into those savings at times to cover the unexpected or under-estimated. But you know what, I am thankful to God for having had the discipline to save because there was money available when needed.

Going forward you may want to adopt a rule like this to follow. The idea is to keep you focused. Personally, I want to improve on what I have been practicing in the past and reduce my spending so I can do more investing. I like this rule better:

- ✓ 10% - Tithe
- ✓ 10% - Save
- ✓ 10% - Invest
- ✓ 70% - Spend (including personal income taxes)

Now it's your turn. Decide how much you want to save. You can either consider adopting a percentage rule or save based on a specified dollar amount for a specific frequency and period. What's your Financial Empowerment Rule? If you don't want to do this right now that's okay. You can continue to the other sections of the workbook and come back to this once you have completed them. No pressure ☺.

My Commitment	Dollar Amount OR Percentage on Gross Income
I will tithe	
I will save	
I will invest	
I will limit my spending to	

Calculate How Much You Can Save

Money saved is money earned. You can gain interest or investment income on what you saved. Or you can save money by paying cash for an item rather than purchasing it on credit.

What if you paid yourself at least $50 each month for 20 years at a meager 2% interest? You would earn $2,739.84 more in interest.

Gross monthly salary	$2,500.00
2% of monthly amount	50.00
Value After 20 years @ 2% interest	$14,764.41
Total Invested (in 20 years)	12,000.00
Interest earned	$2,764.41

That may seem like a small amount after 20 years, but the most important aspect of this habit of paying yourself is that you actually have money at your disposal to carry out the assignment you've attached to it. Of course, the more you save, the more interest you will earn. In its simplest form, money does makes money.

Now you work it out for yourself based on your current income, the percentage of your income that you'd like to save, and the estimated interest rate you can expect to receive. For quick calculation of the interest, you can easily search the internet for a Savings Calculator or use a spreadsheet 'Future value' formula to calculate the amount. Alternatively, you can use the Savings Calculator included in the Financial Empowerment Workbook worksheets from my website. Write the numbers in the space below.

Gross monthly salary	
___% of monthly amount	
Value After ___ years @ ___% interest	
Total Invested (in ___ years)	
Interest earned	

I hope this exercise gives you more inspiration to start saving now!

Practical and Fun Ways to Save

In this section, you are going to decide how you will start saving. If you have a plan in of action in place, you are most likely to succeed in reaching your goal. For the options listed below, choose at least two options that you implement immediately. Write in the amount and frequency with which you plan to save. If you can think of other ways to save apart from what is listed below, feel free to use the extra space provided. I would like to hear from you too. Send me a tweet (https://twitter.com/pamvcarmichael) to let me know what saving options you chose and what wins you've gained from this exercise.

Save method	Savings Assignment	Monthly Savings Goal
For example: Payroll deduction to your savings account or register savings account. *Note:* Some employers have a matching program for this type of account. Find out if your employer does.	Golden Years Fund	5% of my gross salary If salary is $2,500 per month, then my savings is $125 per month. If my employer matches who I save, then $250 is saved each month!
Payroll deduction to your savings account or register savings account		
Automatic debit from your checking account to your savings account		
At the end of each week dump all the coins in your wallet into a jar and don't count it until is full		
Save a specific denomination. For example, set aside in a jar each week $1, $5 and stuff that jar until it can't close!		

Calculate how much you would like to save each week or month. Write it down.		
Do you have a treat that you buy every day e.g. coffee, snack bar. Instead of buying make your own coffee and prepare a healthy snack. Put the money you would have spent on these items into a savings account		
Design jars with a specific savings assignment and teach your children to save (and tithe too)		

Think about it: What you see is what you spend. What you have easy access to, you spend. Saving limits the amount of disposal income you have to consume (i.e. dine out, entertainment, frivolous or impulse spending). If you place your savings in an account that is not easily accessible and keep minimal amounts in your main account for daily use, you'll likely spend less and save more.

My Savings Commitment

I, _____ make a commitment to myself and God to implement steps needed build up my savings on a regular basis.

I believe that God will command His blessings on all my storehouses as I walk in obedience to His Word.

I will use my storehouses as He directs to establish the kingdom of God in my life and in the lives of those He inspires me to help. I know that He will keep me in all my ways as I commit all things to Him

Signature: _____   Date: _____

The Lord will command the blessing on you in your storehouses and in all to which you set your hand, and He will bless you in the land which the Lord your God is giving you. – Deuteronomy 28:8 (NKJV)

INVEST: LET MONEY WORK FOR YOU

"He who supplies the investment seed will also multiply it." — Pamela Carmichael

Divide your portion to seven, or even to eight, for you do not know what misfortune may occur on the earth. — Ecclesiastes 11:2 (NASB)

Why Don't You Invest Your Money?

Investing is key to becoming financially empowered. It's a step up from saving for the short-term and therefore requires more discipline, patience and of course professional guidance in order to reap the rewards of financial increase.

If you worked through the exercises on saving, you would quickly realize it takes money to make money. Money attracts money. For most people this is a known fact, but not a lived experience. Why? The average individual does not think they have anything worth investing. In earlier times, investing may have been restricted to the wealthy, but now investment opportunities are more readily available to the masses. Furthermore, investing is often seen as a very risky option due to the crashes in the financial markets and greedy and unscrupulous schemes crafted by those in the financial industry.

Along with these two general reasons for not investing your money wisely to bring financial increase, what other reasons can you identify with? Check the ones that apply to you.

- ☐ The financial markets are complicated. I wouldn't know where to start.
- ☐ I am not sure what investment options are out there. The only thing I know of is the stock market and I'm not interested in going there.
- ☐ I barely have enough to save, I can think about investing now!
- ☐ I lack investment knowledge.
- ☐ I think I would lose my money. It's hard to tell what a good investment is these days.
- ☐ There is too much work involved in investing—too much research—and there are no guarantees either.
- ☐ That's for rich people, not me.
- ☐ I am drowning in debt. I will have to put off investing until I get this debt paid off.
- ☐ I'd rather keep my money under a mattress than invest in anything. There's just too much

risk all round.

☐ I've been burned already. Lost a lot of money. I cannot risk my money like that again.

If you can think of some other reason for not investing, write it down here:

_____

_____

_____

_____

_____

The Benefits of Investing: A Biblical View

Please don't let these reasons deter you from making good, sound and socially responsible investments. Truth be told, though investing can have its highs and lows, the job is doable with God's direction and the help of a sound financial professional.

Did you get what I said though, take this and any other life decision with God's direction. Proverbs 3:5–6 is not a cliché—don't leave God out of whatever investment decisions you make.

Trust in and rely confidently on the Lord with all your heart and do not rely on your own insight or understanding. In all your ways know and acknowledge and recognize Him, and He will make your paths straight and smooth [removing obstacles that block your way]. – Proverbs 3:5-6 (AMP)

Let's work at renewing your thinking if you have any hesitation about making investments. *Financial Empowerment: Realign Your Finances to God's Will* (https://www.amazon.com/dp/B00AQXMAT0) gives several good reasons why investing is a good financial practice. I encourage you to research, read books, or talk to financial professionals. You will find more than enough documented support that would justify and confirm the benefits of investing.

For each of the following statements I have noted just one Bible verse that speaks to investing. Can you find more at least one more? Write one in the space provided.

But take note of the word of God that ministers to you. What do I mean? You may be at a stage in your life where you are focused on your children and you want them to be well taken care of when you've left this earth. Maybe the scripture on leaving an inheritance is what you need to focus on.

✓ Money attracts money.

Matthew 25:29 - For to everyone who has, more will be given, and he will have abundance; but from him who does not have, even what he has will be taken away.

_____

_____

_____

_____

_____

✓ Invest to leave an inheritance.

Proverbs 13:22a - A good man leaves an inheritance to his children's children.

_____

_____

_____

_____

_____

✓ Invest for your present and future needs. Yes, God too anticipates your present and future needs.

Leviticus 25: 21-22 – I will send you such a blessing in the sixth year that the land will yield enough for three years. While you plant during the eighth year, you will eat from the old crop and will continue to eat from it until the harvest of the ninth year comes in.

_____

_____

_____

_____

_____

✓ When you have wealth you can freely bless others and promote the kingdom of God.

2 Corinthians 9:8 (AMPC) - _And God is able to make all grace (every favor and earthly blessing) come to you in abundance, so that you may always and under all circumstances and whatever the need be self-sufficient_ [possessing enough to require no aid or support and furnished in abundance for

every good work and charitable donation].

_____

_____

_____

_____

_____

Investing is not for the lazy or fearful. Read Matthew 25:14-30 to understand what I mean by that statement. It requires time and hard work. You have to manage it. For God that's being faithful. Once you are faithful, He will reward beyond what you could even imagine. Investment of money (along with your time and effort) will reap a greater return than having your funds in a savings or fixed income account. When you invest, please make sure to:

1. Expect a return on your investment
2. Get professional help
3. Think long term
4. Be cautious and avoid what you're unsure or uncomfortable about
5. Evaluate your portfolio regularly and make adjustments as needed
6. Start investing even a little (if you not have started yet)

Now it's your turn.

You've studied a little on the benefits of investing, but here's an important question for you: Why do you want to invest? Write down a few compelling reasons why it is important for you to take this step.

_____

_____

_____

_____

_____

_____

_____

I hope you were able to clarify for yourself why it is important to invest.

RIGHT NOW, in this present moment it is time to start investing. At the most basic level, saving is the starting point to investing. If you need to, go back and review that section: **Save: Pay Yourself**

Too. However, don't delay, because you won't want to forgo any more returns.

Type of Investments to Consider

To give you clarity I have listed a few different types of investments along with the typical investment horizon needed if you want to experience relatively good returns. Your age as well as your level of risk tolerance to the different types of investments will be significant factors in determining which are best for you. It is at this stage that I encourage you to consider getting the professional help of a qualified investment advisor to aid in your decision making.

Investment opportunities generally fit into two categories (1) ownership, in which case you earn a return on your investment in the form of profit or dividends or (2) lending, in which case your earn interest on the money lent. You may be more familiar with the ownership aspect of investing, but lending is another form of investing worth consideration. This type of lending—like lending to the poor which is good and has great returns beyond monetary gain—can be God-honouring if you take care and responsibility for where your money goes.

Type of Investment	Typical Duration For Good Returns
☐ Savings/Cash Account – typically used for reserve or emergency fund	Short term – less than 1 year
☐ Invest in yourself – Develop a new skill or improve skills you already have. Then sell your services. This is one of the best kinds of investments you can make! ☺	Lifetime
☐ Insurance policies with cash values – this type of investment is beneficial at a young age since it proves cost effect then. The benefit here is that your life is covered and you are building a cash reserve at the same time. These policies are good even for babes and school age children to save for future education.	Lifetime

☐ Insurance policies without cash values – This isn't really an investment. It's more like risk coverage. I call it an instant estate. If you have minimal savings and a family to care for, consider an insurance policy to cover debt and funeral expenses. This is a way of caring for your family and their future.	Lifetime
☐ Registered Education Savings Plan	5 years or more
☐ Registered Retirement Savings Plan	Lifetime investment
☐ Fixed Income Accounts	1 to 5 years
☐ Bonds – a form of lending to corporations, governments or other entities	5 years or more
☐ Peer-to-peer Lending Account – another form of lending but typically to individuals and small entities	3 to 5 years or longer depending on the terms of the loans invested in
☐ Stocks – gives you a fraction of ownership in a publicly traded company	5 years or more
☐ Mutual Funds – A collection of stocks and/or bonds (and possibly other investments)	5 years or more
☐ Real Estate– This is directly investing in properties. You become a landlord. Either buy and rent a house or rent part of your current house. Alternatively, you can buy, fix and flip (i.e. sell) the house and make a substantial profit.	15 – 30 years based on mortgage terms

☐ Real Estate Investment Trusts (REITs) – Real estate is directly investing in properties. However a REIT is company that owns, operates or finances income-producing real estate. You can invest either by purchasing the stock of the company or mutual funds that specialize in public real estate.	5 years or more
☐ New Business Venture – you may invest in your own business or partner with someone	This is certainly a long term investment – 5 years or more
☐ Alternative Investments – these could be hedge funds or other high risk investment. This type if investing is marketed to high net worth individuals.	5 years or more

Taking a Faith Step: My Commitment to Invest

Since you're making a NOW move to invest, the next question is how much, for how long, and for what purpose. The truth is, you're the only one who can answer those questions.

Determine an amount that you feel comfortable investing on a regular basis (weekly or monthly at the most). Fill out the commitment form and contact a financial service professional to assist you in placing your funds wisely.

MY INVESTMENT PROMISE

Today, I will invest $_____ on a (weekly, monthly, quarterly) basis into
_____ (name of account or specific investment).

The purpose or assignment of this/these investment(s) is to save towards:

☐ My golden years

☐ An education fund for my child _____ (name of child)

☐ _____ (other purpose)

Lord, I place these funds in your care and I ask that You command increasing returns as I faithfully commit to doing this.

Signature: _____   Date: _____

The Lord will command the blessing on you in your storehouses and in all to which you set your hand, and He will bless you in the land which the Lord your God is giving you. – Deuteronomy 28:8

The Lord will open to you His good treasure, the heavens, to give the rain to your land in its season, and to bless all the work of your hand. You shall lend to many nations, but you shall not borrow. — Deuteronomy 28:12

SPEND: DON'T BUY EVERY GOOD-BUY

"Does excessive spending benefit your economy?" — Pamela Carmichael

What Type of Spender Are You?

In *Financial Empowerment: Realign Your Finances to God's Will* (https://www.amazon.com/dp/B00AQXMAT0) I talk about the 'Consume Me' age we are living in and the impact it has on how we manage and spend money. This consumer-driven society has caused many to develop an 'I-want-it-now' mindset that causes havoc on their financial situation. The pull of external influences (friends, family members, work colleagues, neighbours, advertising, etc.) coupled with your own self-talk or perception about money, affect how you spend money and by extension manage it.

In this session, we need to take a closer look at your spending patterns and work out how those that have a negative impact on your finances can be addressed. First, you need to identify what kind of spender you are. Check off from the list below any statements that apply to how your approach spending your money.

Spending Thought / Statement	Type of Spender
☐ I buy what I need.	Essentials
☐ I must have the best and the latest.	Extravagant
☐ I want one like his/hers.	Covetous
☐ I worked hard so I deserve it.	Entitlement
☐ I feel a bit down today so I need to treat myself a little retail therapy.	Emotional
☐ I earned it so whatever else is needed will have to wait.	Egotistic / Selfish
☐ I shop till I drop. (I.e. too tired and too broke).	Exhausted / Drained
☐ If I like it, I buy it.	Emotional
☐ All my friends have so why can't I too? (i.e. I don't want to be left out).	Envious
☐ It's the new in thing.	Extravagant

☐ I just gotta have it, I don't care what anybody thinks or how much it costs.	Extravagant
☐ I thought it would be a good thing to have, so I bought it. But now I don't use it.	Emotional
☐ Relax, have fun! What's the point of having money if you can't spend it?	Extravagant

Can you think of any other statements you have expressed (in thought or in action) about how you should spend your money? Write them down.

_____

_____

_____

_____

_____

_____

Scriptural Help and Healing for the Big Spender

You know yourself. Furthermore, God knows you even better. Are you a big spender? Or do you spend just what you should but still need to get a handle on your finances? Regardless of where you are at, this workbook can help you address your money challenges.

If you are a big spender there is hope to curb the spending. If you think you are spending the bare minimum but are still in financial straits, that can be dealt with as well.

Essentials	Sometimes, you need to be content with what you have and just spend on the basics. *"I am not saying this because I am in need, for I have learned to be content whatever the circumstances. I know what it is to be in need, and I know what it is to have plenty. I have learned the secret of being content in any and every situation, whether well fed or hungry, whether living in plenty or in want."* — Philippians 4:11–12 (NIV)
Extravagant	You need self-control to curb the spending habit. Ask the Lord Jesus for help in this area. *"For God gave us a spirit not of fear but of power and love and self-control.* —2 Timothy 1:7 (ESV)
Covetous / Envious	Buying an item out of envy shows the condition of your heart. Guard your heart. *"For from within, [that is] out of the hearts of men, come base and wicked thoughts, sexual immorality, stealing, murder, adultery, coveting (a greedy desire to have more wealth), dangerous and destructive wickedness, deceit;* [a]*unrestrained (indecent) conduct; an evil eye (envy), slander (evil speaking, malicious misrepresentation, abusiveness), pride (*[b]*the sin of an uplifted heart against God and man), foolishness (folly, lack of sense, recklessness, thoughtlessness). All these evil* [purposes and desires] *come from within, and they make the man unclean and render him unhallowed."*— Mark 7:21-23 (AMPC)
Entitlement	Entitlement happens when you think you deserve money even without working to earn it and have received too much too soon. Money or the spirit of mammon can give you a false sense of pride and security. You have money and you think you always have, so you spend carelessly without any thought of the future. Read Luke 15:11-32

Emotional	Oftentimes, when you don't let your emotions get the most of you, you'd realized that what you thought you needed you don't need at all. *"For which of you, desiring to build a tower, does not first sit down and count the cost, whether he has enough to complete it?"*— Luke 14:28 (ESV)
Egotistic / Selfish	Being selfish is not a godly characteristic and it can show up in how you spend just as much as how you pray! *"[Or] you do ask [God for them] and yet fail to receive, because you ask with wrong purpose and evil, selfish motives. Your intention is [when you get what you desire] to spend it in sensual pleasures."* — James 4:3 (AMPC)
Exhausted / Drained	A carefree or callous attitude towards money can lead you to shopping sprees that were unplanned or uncalled for. This kind of spender often is exhausted mentally and emotionally and drained financially and usually has high debt. Read Luke 15:11-32

These words above point more to the condition rather than the solution, but if you did read Luke 15-11-32 you will find the answer to solving the spending problem.

1. Come to your senses. Recognize how excessive spending does not help you at all. One question you can ask yourself is: Whose economy am I boosting when I do extreme spending? I think the answer is obvious, don't you?
2. Repent. Ask God for forgiveness. Also consider those you care for, because you may have put them under undue stress because of your spending habits.

Write out a short prayer asking God for forgiveness regarding any negative spending habits you have developed. Don't forget that God's grace is sufficient to help you overcome any weakness.

_____

_____

_____

_____

_____

_____

_____

_____

_____

_____

_____

_____

_____

_____

Expense Tracking Exercises

Now that you have addressed the heart matter of spending, it's time to move onto some practical ways to keep your spending under wraps.

One way to start doing this is to learn what you are currently doing with your money on a daily basis. In this exercise, I want you to (1) get a small note book to record what you are buying daily OR (2) print out a copy of the **Expense Tracking Worksheet** below and record your spending activity. You will need to do this for at least two weeks to a month.

Consider all of the following expense types when tracking. Don't leave anything out.

Apartment or House Rent	Gas: Vehicle	Medical Care
Bank Charges	Groceries	Mortgage
Cell Phone Service	Insurance: Health	Personal Care: Hair care
Clothing	Insurance: House	Personal Care: Spa
Credit Card Payments	Insurance: Life	School Expenses
Dental Care	Insurance: Vehicle	Telephone
Electricity	Internet	Television Subscription
Entertainment	Loan or least Payment: Vehicle	Water

Here are the steps to track your spending:

1. Record all spending regardless of payment method used
2. Payment method short Codes:
   - Cash - C
   - Debit - D
   - Visa - V
   - MasterCard – MC
   - American Express - AMEX
3. If possible, make note of the expense at the time of purchase. If you are unable to do this then make sure to get the receipt and write in the details at the end of each day.
4. At the end of the tracking period (i.e. two weeks to a month), review your expense tracking record.

Expense Tracking Worksheet

Date	Where	Category	Amount	Pymt method

How much can you save if you spend less?

Consider the following questions when you review your Expense Tracking Worksheet:

Were there any consistent or repeated purchases e.g. coffee, snacks, lunch, dinners or social outings?

_____

_____

_____

_____

_____

_____

Can any of the repeated purchases be eliminated or reduced to save money? If so, how much would I save if I did spend on these items anymore? e.g. If you bought lunch 5 days a week for average of $20 per lunch. You would save $80 if you bought lunch once a week and instead took your left-over dinners, salad or sandwich with you instead. Now you try and see how much you can save if you don't spend on certain items.

_____

_____

_____

_____

_____

Apart from the repeated spending patterns, are there any other expenses that can be reduced or eliminated? e.g. investigate your options to reduce the cost of TV, internet, cell phone, even vehicle insurance, etc. if you switch service providers or remove service for period of time if you don't really need or use it. Again, calculate those amounts you don't need to spend on a weekly or monthly basis.

(Personal note: I removed my television subscription. The monthly cost wasn't worth it since my family is rather busy with work and school and we hardly watch television when we are at home anyway. Plus, who can watch so many channels? Think about it.)

_____

_____

_____

_____

_____

What other benefits can I receive from these expense reductions? Note what applies and show the amounts you could use towards these improvements:

Benefit of reducing expenses	Amount per week or month
Improve my cash flow	
Save towards my freedom fund (3-6 month living expenses)	
Save the amount towards a specific goal e.g. travel, gift or upcoming celebration	
Invest in myself – personal development or other training	

Complete a Spending Plan

Knowing what you do with your money on a weekly, monthly, quarterly and annual basis is important. If you plan what you do with the money, you will encounter little or no financial surprises or issues.

This exercise will require some effort on your part to complete, but is well worth it. You will need to collect the following in order to start filling in the Spending Plan (or Cash Flow statement) below:

- Income records – pay slips or other records showing additional income sources
- Bills and agreements – these may be weekly, monthly, quarterly, or annual payments
- Credit cards statements – for now the minimum payment amounts should be noted
- Estimate of adhoc expenses – an expense that does occur regularly e.g. vehicle repairs

The purpose of this is to determine what your net monthly cash balance should be in your main checking account once all income and expense items are accounted for. Of course, you should have separate accounts for all your savings and investments.

SPENDING PLAN – FIRST 6 MONTHS	Jan	Feb	March	Apr	May	June	½ Year TOTALS
GROSS INCOME							
Income Taxes							
Social Insurance Deduction							
Other – Taxes or Required Deductions							
Net Salary							
Other Deductions							
Retirement Savings Plan							
Health Insurance							
Other – Personal Deductions							
Net Other Deductions							
Net Salary Received at Bank							
EXPENSES							
Tithe							
Offerings							
Savings – Freedom Fund							

SPENDING PLAN – FIRST 6 MONTHS	Jan	Feb	March	Apr	May	June	½ Year TOTALS
Savings – Other							
Investments							
Life Insurance							
Mortgage / House Rent							
House Insurance							
Real Estate Taxes							
Electricity							
Water							
Internet							
Telephone							
Television Subscription							
Car Payment							
Car Insurance							
Road Taxes							
Car Maintenance							
Car Gas							
Groceries							
Bank Charges							
Cash In Hand							

SPENDING PLAN – FIRST 6 MONTHS	Jan	Feb	March	Apr	May	June	½ Year TOTALS
Dental Care							
Medical Care							
Cell Phone Service							
Entertainment							
School Expenses							
Family Vacation							
Other Expenses							
Credit Card Payments							
Debt Reduction							
Personal Care							
Clothing							
Other Expenses							
Total Expenses							
NET CASH FLOW							
OTHER INCOME							

SPENDING PLAN – FIRST 6 MONTHS	Jan	Feb	March	Apr	May	June	½ Year TOTALS
Other Income #1							
Other Income #2							
Tithe							
Donations / Giving							
Net Other Income Streams							
TOTAL NET CASH FLOW + NET OTHER INCOME							

SPENDING PLAN – SECOND 6 MONTHS	Jul	Aug	Sep	Oct	Nov	Dec	2nd ½ Year TOTALS
GROSS INCOME							
Income Taxes							
Social Insurance Deduction							
Other – Taxes or Required Deductions							
Net Salary							
Other Deductions							
Retirement Savings Plan							
Health Insurance							
Other – Personal Deductions							
Net Other Deductions							
Net Salary Received at Bank							
EXPENSES							
Tithe							
Offerings							

SPENDING PLAN – SECOND 6 MONTHS	Jul	Aug	Sep	Oct	Nov	Dec	2nd ½ Year TOTALS
Savings – Freedom Fund							
Savings – Other							
Investments							
Life Insurance							
Mortgage / House Rent							
House Insurance							
Real Estate Taxes							
Electricity							
Water							
Internet							
Telephone							
Television Subscription							
Car Payment							
Car Insurance							
Road Taxes							
Car Maintenance							
Car Gas							
Groceries							
Bank Charges							
Cash In Hand							

SPENDING PLAN – SECOND 6 MONTHS	Jul	Aug	Sep	Oct	Nov	Dec	2nd ½ Year TOTALS
Dental Care							
Medical Care							
Cell Phone Service							
Entertainment							
School Expenses							
Family Vacation							
Other Expenses							
Credit Card Payments							
Debt Reduction							
Personal Care							
Clothing							
Other Expenses							
Total Expenses							
NET CASH FLOW							
OTHER INCOME							
Other Income #1							
Other Income #2							
Tithe							
Donations / Giving							

SPENDING PLAN – SECOND 6 MONTHS	Jul	Aug	Sep	Oct	Nov	Dec	2nd ½ Year TOTALS
Net Other Income Streams							
TOTAL NET CASH FLOW + NET OTHER INCOME							

Spend-Less Tips

I hope you were able to complete the Spending Plan. Every day there is a constant need to decide if to spend or not to spend. Try this exercise when you think you're going to break your spending plan

☐ Give yourself a temporary retail therapy. What do I mean by that? If there's something in the store you like and you still have more shopping to do (for the needed items), walk around the store with the item for a few minutes. Then before you go to the cashier, put the item back! (Please do this only if you think you are strong enough to handle it, or if you have the support of a friend who will remind you to put the item back.)

☐ Walk with cash and leave the debit and credit cards at home or in the car. That way, you can only pay with what you have available.

☐ Take inventory of your groceries before going to the store. Make a list of what you need before going to the store.

☐ Question yourself: Do I really need to have this now? Wait 24 hours. If you see an item that isn't part of your money plan for the month, make a U-turn out of the store and even tell the store assistant that you'll think about it.

☐ Adopt the attitude that you don't need to buy everything you see in the shopping window or make a decision before you go to the store that you won't be buying anything you didn't plan for.

☐ Rearrange your mindset. Instead of thinking immediately about what you should spend on when you receive, think first about what you should give and save instead.

☐ Received a gift or extra income? Wait a few days before doing anything with it. If you received cash, leave it at home in safekeeping or deposit it to a savings account.

☐ Keep your goals in mind. If you have a big ticket item that you're saving towards, post an image of it on your phone or computer desktop as a reminder.

☐ Avoid shopping with friends who like to shop a lot. Get an accountability partner or two— those who would keep you in check when they see you're about to break your bank account.

Can you think of anything else you can do to make sure you don't spend any more than you should? Make a note of other ideas here and refer back to the other Spend-Less Tips above whenever you need to.

Above all the tips and suggestions, the one tip that has kept me from over spending is this:
I asked the Lord to remove my desire for buying what I don't need or can't afford to buy.
Trust me, He will do just the same for you!

THE SPENDER'S PRAYER

Lord, I give You praise. I thank You. You have been my Faithful God, Father - Ultimate Source – every day of my life! You are my Provider.

Lord, let your kingdom come and your will be done in me! Help me to effectively manage my finances. I admit that I sometimes (or often) overspend. My spending habits have resulted in me being in debt, stressed out and very unhappy about my financial situation. Now I want to change that. Lord, I need your help.

Father, forgive me for spending unnecessarily and creating financial difficulties in my life and for my family that could have been avoided. Give me the ability to say NO to spending temptations. Help me to think and act wisely – to spend judiciously, invest sensibly and give fearlessly. Don't allow me to be motivated by selfishness or a desire to impress others. Rather, in all I do let it be done out of a genuine love for you and others.

Thank you for forgiving me and embracing me as your child. May I never take for granted any of your blessings, but help me to appreciate all you do and to share with others. Let your kingdom come and your will be done in every area of my life. All honour and glory to you forever! Let it be done, in Jesus' Name.

GIVE: INVEST IN OTHERS

"You can always have a valid reason for not giving. Give anyway." — Pamela Carmichael

"For if you give, you will get! Your gift will return to you in full and overflowing measure, pressed down, shaken together to make room for more, and running over. Whatever measure you use to give—large or small—will be used to measure what is given back to you." — Luke 6:38 (TLB)

I really like these words of David in 1 Chronicles 29:14b (MSG) "Everything comes from you; all we're doing is giving back what we've been given from your generous hand." Yes I know; I know you've heard enough about giving already. Regardless of where you go—church, home, work, shopping mall, grocery store—there is a constant request from others "Please give." You might even say you've had enough of giving, but really, have you? David's words constantly ring through my mind whenever the opportunity to give is presented. We can only give what we have been given, and God is generous, and from His gifts to us we can only give back to Him and others accordingly.

If that is the case, then why do you find it hard to give at times? What are your challenges as it relates to giving?

What's holding you back?

Are you a generous person? Giving is the heart of God. He gave His son for you and me so that we can lay hold of an abundant life here and now and for eternity. He gives you what you need for each day and even for your heart's desires. Romans 8:32 (TLB), *"Since he did not spare even his own Son for us but gave him up for us all,* **won't he also surely give us everything else?"**

As God's child, as His representative here in the earth, you should reflect His heart in your life and therefore being generous should be you. However, it is understandable that giving can sometimes be a challenge. If that is the case for you, let's identify what is holding you back from giving. Which of these statements applies to you?

- ☐ I give but sometimes I don't give as much as I can.
- ☐ I don't have the heart to give. I just do it because I am expected to.
- ☐ What if I give too much and then when I need I don't have.

- ☐ I don't believe that giving is a blessing. I don't see these "blessings" coming to me anyways.
- ☐ I don't tithe, but I give when I feel like it.
- ☐ I have too many responsibilities. I barely have anything left over to give.
- ☐ I see people in need and I really wish I have more so I could help them.
- ☐ Everybody wants something these days—churches, other charitable organizations, all types of causes—they don't seem to think that I need gifts too!
- ☐ Sometimes I worry if I'd have enough for the unexpected,
- ☐ I just give what I can when I can. I don't plan what to give.

Can you identify with any of these statements? If you can think of anything else that has kept you from being a generous person, write it down.

_____

_____

_____

_____

_____

_____

Most of these statements point to the heart condition or the mind-set you have towards giving. In some cases, these statements confirm your ability or willingness to give or not to give because of personal circumstances in your life. As is often said, the hardest part is to know—if you know your challenges, then you can work to address them. In the next few sections, you will work to understanding the how-to's of giving along with the benefits of giving and determine what you can do start or to improve the practice of consistent, cheerful giving.

As you do these steps, you may feel the need to ask the Lord Jesus to forgive you in some areas or to help you overcome any obstacles that have been hindering you from giving, whether it is a heart issue or a financial one. Be sure to ask and thank God for the grace to become a cheerful giver.

The Biblical Basis of Giving: How To Fearlessly Give

Let's move forward to study the benefits of giving and how you should give. In this section, I want you to take time out the review and study the Bible verses provided below. Next to each verse, please complete the fill-in-the-blank statement. You can meditate on these personal statements regularly to help you develop the mind and the heart of a cheerful giver.

Giving Scriptures	Personal Statement of Giving
2 Corinthians 9:6 AMPC [Remember] *this: he who sows sparingly and grudgingly will also reap sparingly and grudgingly, and he who sows generously* [*that blessings may come to someone*] *will also reap generously and with blessings.*	What I give is connected to what I r_____ or reap.
2 Corinthians 9:7 AMPC *Let each one* [give] *as he has made up his own mind and purposed in his heart, not reluctantly or sorrowfully or under compulsion, for God loves (He takes pleasure in, prizes above other things, and is unwilling to abandon or to do without) a cheerful (joyous, 'prompt to do it') giver* [*whose heart is in his giving*].	God wants me to make up my m_____ to give and to do so with a j_____ heart.
2 Corinthians 8:3 AMPC *For, as I can bear witness,* [*they gave*] *according to their ability, yes, and beyond their ability; and* [*they did it*] *voluntarily*	There are times I might need to give above and beyond. I may give sac_____ly.
Matthew 6: 25-34 *Therefore I tell you, stop being perpetually uneasy (anxious and worried) about your life, what you shall eat or what you shall drink; or about your body, what you shall put on. Is not life greater* [*in quality*] *than food, and the body* [*far above and more excellent*] *than clothing.*	I should not give in fear or worry about lacking anything. God always p_____ whatever I need.
Acts 20:35 *I have shown you in every way, by laboring like this, that you must support the weak. And remember the words of the Lord Jesus, that He said, 'It is more blessed to give than to receive.'"*	Jesus said it, so I accept and believe. I am more b_____ when I give than when I receive.

Proverbs 19:17 *He who has pity on the poor lends to the Lord, and that which he has given He will repay to him.*	When I give to others, I am l_____ to the Lord who will more than adequately repay me.
Malachi 3:8 *Will a man rob or defraud God? Yet you rob and defraud Me. But you say, In what way do we rob or defraud You? [You have withheld your] tithes and offerings.*	From now on, I shall not be found guilty of robbing or d_____ God by withholding what is rightfully His – tithes and of_____.
2 Corinthians 9:10 AMPC *And [God] Who provides seed for the sower and bread for eating will also provide and multiply your [resources for] sowing and increase the fruits of your righteousness [which manifests itself in active goodness, kindness, and charity].*	My God is able to multiple my r_____ which are made more available to me to give good gifts.
2 Corinthians 9:8 AMPC *And God is able to make all grace (every favor and earthly blessing) come to you in abundance, so that you may always and under all circumstances and whatever the need be self-sufficient [possessing enough to require no aid or support and furnished in abundance for every good work and charitable donation].*	No matter how great the needs of others are God will provide s_____ to me so I can give toward every g_____ work that is presented to me.
Proverbs 11:24 AMPC *There are those who [generously] scatter abroad, and yet increase more; there are those who withhold more than is fitting or what is justly due, but it results only in want.* **Luke 6:38** *Give, and it will be given to you: good measure, pressed down, shaken together, and running over will be put into your bosom. For with the same measure that you use, it will be measured back to you.*	I should **fearlessly** give knowing that when I give I will r_____ and have more than I gave.

1 Corinthians 16:2 *On the first [day] of each week, let each one of you [personally] put aside something and save it up as he has prospered [in proportion to what he is given], so that no collections will need to be taken after I come.*	Giving shouldn't always be spontaneous, I should p_____ what I am going to give.
2 Corinthians 9:7 *So let each one give as he purposes in his heart, not grudgingly or of necessity; for God loves a cheerful giver.*	God wants me to have the right attitude towards giving. I should be _____ and _____ when I give.

How much are you willing to give?

"Start giving. No matter how small the amount might be, commit to giving on a regular basis to a charity of your choice, to your local church mission, or even to a child-sponsorship program. To ensure you do, set up a preauthorized payment plan. Watch and see how blessed you will be just by knowing you're making a difference in someone else's life. Your giving to someone has eternal value." — Pamela Carmichael, Financial Empowerment

As the above quota says, start giving. When I prepare my estimated cash flows for a specific period I include a percentage of my income as part of my offering or giving. In other words, I set a giving budget. You can consider starting with 1% of your income and work your way up from there.

Some biblical financial professionals recommend having an account or fund to deposit this gift money so that when the need arises you don't have to worry about if you can and cannot. Since the money is set aside consistently, you can easily access the funds needed. If there isn't enough, you can give what you can and even give more from your regular bank account if the Lord instructs you to do so and as you desire to.

Below I have created a commitment form. I encourage you to think about and pray about how much you can give and to whom you should give. Once you've decided, complete the commitment and keep it readily available as a reminder of your commitment to the Lord regarding giving.

My Commitment to Fearlessly Give

I commit to giving $_____ or _____% of my income on a weekly or monthly basis to various needs including:

1. _____
2. _____
3. _____
4. _____

I will give consistently, regularly, purposefully, systematically, in proportion to my income and at times above and beyond what I normally give. Certainly, I will give from the heart - lovingly and joyfully.

I am confident that as I give, God will supply abundantly, copiously, plentifully, richly, profusely, lavishly, amply, every need in my life according to His riches in glory by Christ Jesus.

Signature: _____ Date: _____

"For if you give, you will get! Your gift will return to you in full and overflowing measure, pressed down, shaken together to make room for more, and running over. Whatever measure you use to give—large or small—will be used to measure what is given back to you." — Luke 6:38 (TLB)

Practical Ways to Give – Ideas of How You Can Give

You may be silently asking "Is giving always about money?" Of course not. Giving goes beyond the act of donating money. Yes, a monetary gift is practical, especially when supporting hospitals, charities or non-governmental organizations who provide specific and specialized aid and who can determine how best to manage and distribute the funds. The reality is, your money can go places and help others where you cannot practically go and where you don't have the expertise to provide hands-on help. You can be an agent of blessing through giving financial aid. The key to doing this well is to ask God for guidance and to do research to ensure that your contribution is being appropriated wisely.

However, you can consider these ways of giving to add to your financial giving. Check one or two of these that you can do now and consider what you can practice on a regular basis:

☐ **Donate your clothes or other items.** Do you have clothes in good condition that you don't wear or have never worn? Declutter your closet and give them to a friend or your local church or Salvation Army or other charitable organization that receives and distributes to those who need.

☐ **Provide a meal.** Do you know someone in need or a single parent that could do with some help preparing healthful and fun meals for his/her children? Then invite them over for dinner and take a few of your special dishes over to them. I am sure they would appreciate the help.

☐ **Pay for the other person's food bill.** There are two ways to do this: (1) while in the grocery, coffee shop or even a restaurant, pay for the person ahead of or behind you in the line or (2) empty your pantry of the excess or the items you haven't used (before expiry date please!). Simple acts of giving like this will make someone's day and remind them of the goodness of others and of God.

☐ **Volunteer at your church or other charitable organization.** Your time, your skill or experience might prove valuable to some (even more so) than a monetary gift. Consider your interests as well as the needs of several charities and offer yourself as the gift! "*Each of you should use whatever gift you have received to serve others, as faithful stewards of God's grace in its various forms. If anyone speaks, they should do so as one who speaks the very words of God. If anyone serves, they should do so with the strength God provides, so that in all things God may be praised through Jesus Christ.* (1 Peter 4:10-11, NIV)

☐ **Babysit for free!** Offer to take care of someone's children for a few hours while they take a much needed break and have a date night with their spouse.

☐ **Open your home to someone** who is visiting your area, for example, a speaker or pastor attending an event at your church or in the area. Consider offering a friend a mini-staycation. For example, while you are away from home you could open your door for someone to stay there. They may think that you just want them to house-sit but even if that's a benefit for you, to the other person the change of scenery might be just what they need. If you are comfortable doing this, leave your friend with a few ground rules and a full pantry and fridge so they can have a feast! Alternatively, invite a friend or family over for a few days and treat them to a mini bed-and-breakfast package.

☐ **Become a Missionary.** Go on a short-term (or long-term, if you see the need to) mission with your church or other organization. Being out in the field doing hands-on work helps you to understand more clearly the great needs to be addressed. You can quickly appreciate that your lack is not as great as others. You will become more thankful and have an even greater desire to serve and to give more.

☐ **Share the Good News!** The Ultimate and best gift to give is Jesus. At every given opportunity tell others about God's love and His precious gift that keeps on giving—Jesus!

What Can Your Gift Do?

It is wonderful to actually give to someone else. I want you to relish in the fact that you are better off being the giver than the receiver. Get excited about giving instead of feeling that you are losing when you give; consider all that being a cheerful giver does in your life and in other people. Giving has a rippling effect.

Below is a list of statements about what your gift can do. Following is a list of biblical references. For each statement match at least one biblical reference. Write in the space next to the statement. **Hint**: A reference may be used for more than one statement.

Giving ...	Biblical Reference
Creates a void which God will by all means refill for you. On account of your giving, God will copiously provide for you from His unlimited resources.	
Is not a one-sided act. It benefits both the giver and the recipient.	
Blesses beyond your generation.	
Brings wisdom and riches.	
Brings life again.	
Brings salvation to you and yours.	
Refreshes you—God heals the giver.	
Opens the door for you to receive more than you've given.	

Makes you richer or wealthier even though you initially appear to have less.	
Is an investment with a consistent positive return.	
Leads to much needed friendships and/or favour.	
Will cause others to praise to God.	
Makes you happier than receiving.	
Cause you to empower others. (God gives to you that you may give to others.)	

List of giving scriptures:

1 Kings 17:8-16	2 Cor. 9: 11-15	Acts 9:36-42	Matt. 5:16
1 Kings 3:3-15	2 Sam 7:1-17	Luke 16:9	Prov. 11:24 (a)
2 Cor. 9:8-10	Acts 10:1-8	Luke 6:38 (AMP)	Ps. 41:1-3
2 Cor. 8:1-4	Acts 20:35	Mark 12: 41-44	

If you're not convinced yet, I don't know what will. Personally, I see the blessedness of giving daily. Being able to give (which is sharing) some of what God has provided for me with others causes my heart to praise Him for His provision to me. I am happy knowing that I have been able to help others with the gifts I am able to give. I am happy to see people's joy at receiving (from their facial expressions to their verbal and non-verbal expressions) and their expressed appreciation to God and/or to me for the gift. It is an absolute joy to give.

Below I have listed additional points; how you can give in a way that pleases God.
- Give to those who ask (including when God asks you to give towards His work). - Luke 6:30 NIV
- Give like God gives: out of love for others. - Jn. 3:16, Rom. 8:32
- Recognize and appreciate the Source of your ability to give. - 1 Chronicles 29:14b (MSG)
- Be thankful that you have the ability to give or to be a blessing. - 1 Chronicles 29
- Give willingly and cheerfully because God loves when you are happy to give. - 2 Cor. 9:7
- Plan what you will give out of your regular income and when you receive gifts - 1 Cor. 16:2

- o Determine what your giving budget is and set it aside separately for that purpose.
- ➤ Be open to do good works at any time. When a need arises you will be ready to help and not stress about how you can help. - 2 Cor. 9:8-10
- ➤ Ask God to increase your giving ability - Matt 7:7-11, Lk 11:1-4, Lk 11:5-8
  - o God gives good gifts to those who ask persistently; if your desire is to give and help others, God will open doors for increase.
- ➤ Give like you are giving to God. God owes no one and he will repay you for your kindness – Prov. 19:17
- ➤ When you give, don't broadcast it. Most importantly, your Heavenly Father knows what you are doing and He will reward you. - Matt. 6:1-4

May you be compelled to give above and beyond your normal level of giving and experience the blessedness of fearlessly giving (2 Cor. 8:1-4). Blessings!

DEFEAT DEBT:
CONSIDER ONE OF GOD'S SOLUTIONS

Debt is a hard task master. Aim to be debt-free. — Pamela Carmichael

The rich rules over the poor, and the borrower is servant to the lender. — Proverbs 22:7

For the Lord your God will bless you just as He promised you; you shall lend to many nations, but you shall not borrow; you shall reign over many nations, but they shall not reign over you. — Deuteronomy 15:6

The Weight of Debt

In *Financial Empowerment: Realign Your Finances to God's Will* (https://www.amazon.com/dp/B00AQXMAT0) I discussed how debt can have a negative impact on your life—financially, physically, emotionally, socially and even spiritually. Financial debt can:

- ☐ Enslave you, taxing you with years of recurring payments
- ☐ Reduce your investment, purchasing and giving power
- ☐ Result in stress and health issues
- ☐ Cause you to feel boxed in, confined or distressed and depressed
- ☐ Leave you very discontented or angry with yourself, family and creditors
- ☐ Destroy relationships with your loved ones as well as work and business relationships
- ☐ Hinder your voice or your purpose from being fulfilled
- ☐ Take your focus off the Source and Provider and cause you to worry or be anxious constantly

I don't know what financial shape you are in. You might be saying that, "I can manage the debt that I have." Or you may realize that you need to get a handle on your debt and try to reduce it. Whether you have debt that you consider to be manageable or that is spiraling out of control, debt is still debt. Furthermore, debt even in its manageable state can become quickly unmanageable if your life takes a direction that you didn't anticipate or desire. The bottom line, debt leaves you vulnerable and weak and at the not-so-tender mercies of this world system.

On the other side of debt is financial freedom and that is the position God wants you to be in. Furthermore, he wants you to be free enough to lend to others and to do good work with money. Debt doesn't bring that kind of freedom. If you want to experience and live financially empowered, then take time to go through the following sections. Let us work on managing and eventually eliminating debt from your life!

Why Are You in Debt?

To have debt seems like the norm rather than the exception. Once you reach adulthood, it seems natural to have financial challenges and to borrow more than you'd prefer. The unfortunate reality is that no one really taught you how to manage money or how to plan your future inclusive of money goals. You've been trained to think seriously about what you want to be when you grow up. For the most part, it is thought that once you have figured that out and have reached that career goal then you'll have no money issues. But in life, that doesn't prove to be true. Even persons with the most success in their careers or businesses have financial issues, often the result of mismanagement and too much debt.

But what about you? Do you know why you are in debt? Listed below are several reasons. Stop now and think over your life and financial history. Ask yourself, "How did I get into debt?" Check those statements below that echo what your situation is and write down any other reasons not mentioned below. Remember, knowing why will help you understand how you can eventually reduce or eliminate debt from your life.

- ☐ I guess I have been managing money the way I saw my family did. I do what I know.
- ☐ I spend a lot. I like the feeling I get from buying on sale knowing I made a good buy.
- ☐ Trying to satisfy yourself with external rewards—overspending on things you don't need or really want
- ☐ I've had a few challenges (e.g. accident, job loss) that set me back quite a bit.
- ☐ Our family has had to deal with the long term illness and death of our loved one. We were not prepared for this emotionally or even financially.
- ☐ The cost of living keeps increasing but my income hasn't changed. It's been rough trying to get by and I've had to borrow to keep up with the increasing expenses.
- ☐ When it isn't one thing going wrong it's another. There always seems to be something that needs fixing in the house or the car. I don't seem to ever have enough extra to cover these adhoc costs.

- ☐ I have lost out on not having enough insurance coverage when I have a car accident. The medical expenses and the car cost were more than I was covered for.
- ☐ My business did thrive. I was forced to borrow to meet expenses and eventually I have to close. It left me financially drained.
- ☐ I borrowed some money to make an investment. It was supposed to be a sure thing but I ended up losing the capital and any profit that I'd made.

_____

_____

_____

_____

_____

_____

I hope that you were able to identify where the issues are for you. However, please don't be hard on yourself. Rather I want you to take time to make a decision to give yourself a second chance. God sure is willing to give you one and He is willing to help you break free from debt.

Therefore, leave your concerns with Him and ask for the grace to overcome the obstacles and to become a better manager of the resources He has given to you.

Calculate What You Owe

Do you know how much money you owe to others? You may say "Oh, I just have one credit card, it's not much." Good for you. But is that really all? You need to know where you are to determine how to tackle, manage and reduce that debt load.

Why should you know what you owe? This is another reality check. Again, instead of having an 'idea' of what you owe, you make it real by writing it down. This is not something you can forego or gloss over, you need to know where you are at if you want to start moving forward to where you want to go or be.

You cannot start to effectively plan to get out of debt and become financially empowered without first knowing where you are. In completing the Debt Summary exercise (below), you might realize that you've missed out some of your debt. Go back to **My Financial Position** and update it.

My Debt Summary: How Much Do I Owe?

This form, though simple, will prove to be an eye-opener for you. It will be an effective tool in helping you reduce or eliminate any financial debt you have.

Before you start you will need to collect details on any moneys you owe to others. The list is a starting point and a brain teaser to get you think about who you have to repay:

- Household debt (mortgages, home equity loan, secured line of credit)

- Vehicle lease or loan

- Hire purchase or store credit

- Installment loans e.g. education or personal

- Credit cards

- Debt collections

Once you have gathered that information, take time to complete the Debt Summary below. Make sure to calculate the total amount owed and the total minimum payments due. Don't worry about the Priority column as yet, you will come back to that later once we've reviewed how to reduce your debt.

Who did I borrow from?	Amount owed	Min. Payment	Interest Rate %	Due Date	Estimated Payoff Date	Status of Payments?	Priority

TOTAL DEBT / DEBT PAYMENTS								

God's Get-Out-of-Debt Solution

The account of a woman left with a load of debt and the horrific possibility that if she doesn't pay up her sons will be taken away from her and enslaved in 2 Kings 4 provides us with a guide to getting out of debt. I call it 'God's get-out-of-debt solution'.

If you are familiar with this, you might be thinking to yourself that this is history and somewhat unrealistic, because God intervened in this woman's situation to help her get out of debt. However, I'd say that you and I need God's hand in our lives to help us get of debt too!

I encourage you to take a few minutes to read 2 Kings 4:1-7 once again. Even read it from several translations if you can, and it will certainly bring to light the way out of debt. Below I have summarized just what you can do to get out of debt based solely on 2 Kings 4:1-7, and I have included some steps for you to work through at each stage.

Seek Advice from the Wise or Get Professional Advice

This woman took advice from the prophet. In some cases you might deem it appropriate to do as well. Your pastor or spiritual leader in your church should suffice. Alternatively, you might consider professional advice from a debt counsellor or from a financial planner or money coach. You decide. Below lists persons you can confide in and discuss with what your financial options are in relation to reducing or getting out of debt completely. Make sure to set a time to contact one or two of them.

_____

_____

_____

_____

_____

_____

Examine What You Have

What do you have in your house? More importantly what do you have in you? Refuse to discount anything you have or do. What skill, what knowledge do you have that you can offer to others at a price? What are you passionate about? What would you do happily without being paid for it? (That's key to your purpose and to your provision.)

The woman thought she didn't have anything worthwhile that others would gladly pay for. Interestingly enough, she had a valuable and much needed commodity: oil. What value do you have that others would pay for? If you are not sure, ask God to show you and ask your friends and your family. This does not only apply to starting a side-hustle or business, but you might realize that you can pursue the career path you have always wanted that would bring you the additional income you need.

_____

_____

_____

_____

_____

_____

Now start brainstorming about this. Check the list of income-generating options provided earlier in this workbook - **Wealth Creation Alternatives – Multiple Streams of Income.**

Borrow As Needed to Invest

It seems like a contradiction: you are in, debt but you borrow. The guidance given by the prophet was quite clear. The woman was borrowing what she needed—a lot of vessels—in order to help her produce what she would eventually sell.

I would say take this under advisement. Your venture might require capital that isn't currently available to you. You can borrow money or resources. However, consider that you can get some of what you need for free or for barter. You might exchange your skill for an item or share your knowledge to gain more specialized knowledge in an industry that you are interested in. Consider all your options before borrowing. If you have to borrow, you will need to be sure that you can repay! Therefore you will need to approach this step analytically and aggressively and with faith. You will need to be certain that what you have to offer will indeed generate income and be profitable enough to cover the existing and additional debt and provide for you beyond that.

With that said, consider the types of resources you would need. Will you need to borrow or can they be acquired by means of exchange or free of cost? Start to consider these things.

What do I need to produce?	How can I get this?	Estimated Cost
	Total Estimated Cost:	$

Avoid Distractions

It is very easy to get distracted or to lose sight of your goal—whether that goal is to start a new business, get a higher education, become more skilled at what you do, or even work towards getting out of debt and becoming financially empowered.

The Prophet Elisha told this woman to "shut the door behind you and your sons." At first glance this may seem an unnecessary instruction. But let's be real – it's really easy to get off track from our main purpose if we don't cut out the distractions. If you need to get out of debt and there are certain things you need to do to get there, then you will have to purposely cut out the 'who' or the 'what' that will lead you away from achieving it. This holds true for any goal.

Consider what can be distracting to you, for example, television or social media. Also think about what could cause you to stop working on your goal. For example, friends and family may discourage you from pursuing your goal.

Write down those things that could be distracting and then mark an X through them. Cancel them.

_____
_____
_____
_____
_____
_____

Now, that's done. Determine time and space you will carve out of your schedule to work on your goal. Think of what you can do early in the morning before everyone else wakes up, what you can do during normal business hours and what you can do in the evening.

Day	Early Morning	Business hours	Evening / Late Night
Sunday			
Monday			
Tuesday			
Wednesday			
Thursday			
Friday			
Saturday			

Get Busy Producing!

There is no point thinking and planning out what you want to do and then stopping. You need to get busy producing. Like this woman was instructed to pour out the oil that she had, you need to also pour out what is in you. God put it another way when He blessed Adam and Eve: Be fruitful and multiply.

Once you have determined the time you dedicate to this goal, go for it. And need I say it? Yes: Pray for success!

Get Support

You can't do this work on your own. Involve family in the process of getting out of debt. Let your family know your plans and enlist them in the work to make it happen. Having your family and even a faithful friend or two working alongside you makes it easier to get through the highs and lows of reaching your goal.

Even before you get to the stage of producing, it would be best to discuss your plans with your family. Have them buy-in to the idea so that they can support you and do some of the 'heavy lifting' with you.

Write down when and where and how you will share this with your family. If you don't think your immediate household can assist you, consider which of your friends can help. Also having someone support you in prayer would be an added bonus.

Who can I ask to support me in this venture? When will I discuss this with them?

_____

_____

_____

_____

_____

_____

Sell Your Product or Service

Get the sale. This woman had an immediate target market—her neighbors. Know who your target market is for what you are doing, whether it is for a product or a service or for your expertise and knowledge. Who do you plan to sell to? Get an image of them—gender, age, personality type, location, problems, desires, etc. The more you know what your target market looks like the easier it is to reach them and offer them your gift.

_____

_____

_____

_____

_____

_____

_____

Pay Off Your Debt & Live Debt-Free on the Rest

If you've come this far, you've done the work needed to start paying off the debt. God has given you what you need to become debt-free and has provided for your future.

With any new income stream you can start reducing your debt as follows:

- ☐ Direct the additional income into the following pockets: tithing and debt payments.
  - ○ If you think it possible you can even place a portion of savings. For example, 10% tithe, 5% to 10% savings and 75% to 80% debt payments.
- ☐ Using the **My Debt Summary**, determine which debt balance you will put the extra payment towards first.
  - ○ Do this using the Priority column – 1, 2, 3 etc.
- ☐ Continue making the regular minimum payments on all other debts.
- ☐ Once you have completed payment on the first debt balance, celebrate (without spending or spending too much)!
- ☐ Then funnel the amount used to pay off the first amount plus the minimum payment on the second debt to pay the debt marked second priority on your Debt Summary. Keep paying this until that is paid off as well.
- ☐ Continue this process until you have paid off all debt.
- ☐ Finally, with debts paid in full, determine to live a debt-free life. Aim to live on a cash basis only.

Maintain a Low-Debt or Debt-Free Life

With the extra money that is no longer put towards debt payments, consider what you will do with it. Maybe you will be free to give more, save more, invest more, or even spend cash on something you've always wanted to do. The possibilities can be endless when you are free from debt. Dream a little here about what you can accomplish when debt-free. This might be the impetus you need to get you started on the road to being debt free. When you have positive purpose and passion, there's no telling what you can accomplish.

What will I do with the extra I have once I am debt free? ☺

_____

_____

_____

_____

_____

_____

My Debt Payment Commitment

The main key to reducing debt is financial increase i.e. income generation. This can be achieved by starting a new business, developing a hobby or passion into an income stream, investing your money wisely, changing your job or getting a promotion. Whatever you find that is good, productive and profitable, do it. God will help you make the increase.

But as you can determine by now, financial increase isn't all. You have to develop some disciplines such as reducing spending, saving more and making consistent payments to reduce your debt load. The more you do these things, the less debt you have and the more your financial net worth increases.

Today, make a commitment to God and to yourself. If you have deduced the total amount you can pay toward reducing your debt, bravo! Now ask Jesus, your Helper and Strengthener to give you what it takes to become debt-free.

MY DEBT PAYMENT COMMITMENT

I, _____ make a commitment to God and myself to implement steps needed to reduce my debt (and eventually become debt free).

I promise to think carefully before spending any money and with God's help work toward debt free living.

Signature: _____   Date: _____

The Lord shall open to you His good treasury, the heavens, to give the rain of your land in its season and to bless all the work of your hands; and you shall lend to many nations, but you shall not borrow. – Deuteronomy 28:12 (AMPC)

MAKE A MONEY PLAN

Plan life like you're taking a trip or a vacation: map out all the details of your journey.
— Pamela Carmichael

For I know the thoughts that I think toward you, says the Lord, thoughts of peace and not of evil, to give you a future and a hope. — Jeremiah 29:11

Not everyone likes to plan, for the most part; we'd rather not have to think too hard about the details or the nitty-gritty of life. However, the reality is that a planned life usually proves to be a more successful life. As I mentioned in *Financial Empowerment* (https://www.amazon.com/dp/B00AQXMAT0), the main purpose of planning is to map out the journey to your goal even if there are a few diversions or changes along the way. A plan helps you to keep focussed.

What about you? Do you make plans? Do you have life goals (e.g. education, career, business, relationships, etc.) and financial goals linked to those which will either require a cash outflow or an increase in finances (e.g. savings, investing)? For your finances, do you review on a regular basis your financial goals against what was done? For example, did you achieve your savings goal or perhaps exceed it or come in below your target amount?

I know that these may be tough questions, but they are necessary. If you want to be financially empowered for life, planning is part and parcel of this life goal. If you know that you have lapsed in the area of planning, try to first identify some of the reasons you don't make plans.

Why Don't You Have a Money Plan?

Your money or financial plan is closely linked to your other life plans. As you review this list of 'why-nots' below, consider if you are not planning in any area of your life at all. I also graciously recommend using my goal-setting workbook (https://www.amazon.com/dp/0991785037) if you need help in planning life goals. Now let us look at why you do not plan:

- ☐ Carefree lifestyle: "I don't need to plan. I let life happen as it may."
- ☐ Unbelief: "My goals are too big. I am not sure that I can achieve them."
- ☐ Fear of the unknown: "I don't want to think about it. I plan and then something totally opposite happens."
- ☐ Laziness: "It's too much work to plan anything. That's just too much brain work and it's time consuming."

☐ Fear of failure: "I am afraid that my plans will mock me. That my efforts will be an absolute failure."

☐ Uncertainty about how: "I don't even know the first step to take in planning. I don't know how to or even what would be sensible goals."

Are there any extras? What else stops you from planning financially or for your future as a whole?

_____

_____

_____

_____

_____

_____

Embrace the Power of Planning

This might sound like useless repetition, but the first step to planning anything is to seek God for direction. The word of the Lord says that God knows what plans He has designed for you (Jeremiah 29:11). It gets better though, God doesn't just know what He has planned for you, but He also promises that the plans lead to prosperity. Furthermore, the writer in Proverbs 16:3 (AMPC) say it this way: "*Roll your works upon the Lord* [commit and trust them wholly to Him; He will cause your thoughts to become agreeable to His will, and] *so shall your plans be established and succeed.*"

Wow! What's the aim of the workbook but to help you plan your finances in line with God's will for you! With these promises of success, you can review and meditate on the word of God as it speaks to the power of planning. After this section, I hope that you will be geared up to start making and achieving your money plans and life goals.

In the above section titled **"Why Don't You Have A Money Plan?"** six reasons are listed. Below there are statements and scripture verses that address these concerns. Review this list and try to match or associate them to the why-you-don't-plan statements. Then instead of embracing the negative, attach a positive word about planning to each statement. Use the numbered list below.

The Power of Planning	Positive Statement No.
Be diligent to know the state of your flocks, and look well to your herds; For riches are not forever; does a crown endure to all generations? When the hay is gone, the tender grass shows itself, and herbs of the mountain are gathered in, the lambs will be for your clothing, and the goats [will furnish you] the price of a field. And there will be goats' milk enough for your food, for the food of your household, and for the maintenance of your maids. - Proverbs 27: 23 – 27	
He who observes the wind [and waits for all conditions to be favorable] *will not sow, and he who regards the clouds will not reap. As you know not what is the way of the wind, or how the spirit comes to the bones in the womb of a pregnant woman, even so you know not the work of God, Who does all. In the morning sow your seed, and in the evening withhold not your hands, for you know not which shall prosper, whether this or that, or whether both alike will be good.* - Ecclesiastes 11: 4 – 6	
I can do anything with Christ my Helper and Strengthener. (Phil. 4:13) I move forward in faith – trusting Him. I will not walk in fear thinking I will fail.	
If any of you lacks wisdom [to guide him through a decision or circumstance], *he is to ask of* [our benevolent] *God, who gives to everyone generously and without rebuke or blame, and it will be given to him.* – James 1:5 (AMPC)	
It is great to plan, but it is better to act on those plans or goals. In the doing, you can achieve those goals. The doing takes as much faith as the planning. Otherwise, your plans are faith without action. (See Hebrews 11:6; James 2:24)	
Planning compels you to act instead of waiting for life events to happen to you.	

I have listed a few positive planning statements as a guide.

Negative - I Don't Plan	Positive – I Will Plan
Carefree lifestyle: "I don't need to plan. I let life happens as it may."	1. I need to plan my life. With God's help I will fulfill my purpose.
Unbelief: "My goals are too big. I am not sure that I can achieve them."	2. My goals are in line with God's will for me. I will achieve them! I can do all things through Christ my Strength.
Fear of the unknown: "I don't want to think about it. I plan and then something totally opposite happens."	3. I will stop worrying about what will or won't work and act with faith on the plans I have made.
Laziness: "It's too much work to plan anything. That's just too much brain work and it's time consuming."	4. I will be a diligent planner and I will work my plans with God's help.
Fear of failure: "I am afraid that my plans will mock me. That my efforts will be an absolute failure."	5. I have faith that my plans will succeed. Even when there are times of failure, I will not let those failed moments define me. I have faith in God to bring me success.
Uncertainty about how: "I don't even know the first step to take in planning. I don't know how to or even what would be sensible goals."	6. I will ask God for wisdom and seek the sound counsel of others to learn how to plan and begin to act on those plans.

In the next few sections, you will develop a money management plan that works for you. I will take you through the likely action steps you need to take on a regular basis, but feel free to do what works best for you.

Create a Good Money Management Process

Set up a financial review process for yourself and your family. In my opinion a year is too long to wait before doing any kind of financial review or assessment. Too much can happen in a twelve-month time span. The frequency of your financial management process helps you catch investment opportunities or lost money or expenses that you would have otherwise missed. You can re-adjust and keep on track toward your main goal(s). When it comes to money, handle your life and your family's well-being like a business.

In summary a good money management process includes the doing the following:

- ☐ Annual review of your financial position. Look at the positives and negatives. Compare against prior year(s).
- ☐ Create a financial goals worksheet based on your life goals.
- ☐ Review your annual financial calendar and make sure to include all financial events in your projections.
- ☐ Draft a cash flow plan for the year (or at least the first quarter of the year).
- ☐ Weekly review and update your cash flow.
- ☐ Quarterly assessment of your financial position.
- ☐ Make any adjustments in order to keep on track with your goals.

For these steps you can consider either using a spreadsheet or investing in personal finances software. To-date my preference has been a spreadsheet, especially for my cash flow projections of my checking and credit card accounts.

As you go through this planning process you will get a big picture view of where you are as well as work out how to get to where you want to go.

Review Your Financial Position

I know that dealing with money can feel overwhelming at times. You are faced with the responsibilities and challenges of life and managing money is one major task for which there just isn't enough time or energy to take on. Don't worry, you can and will take one step at a time.

You have been down this road before. In the section **My Financial Position** you made a summary of your assets and liabilities. It is necessary to review this. You may even want to recalculate the figures if there has been significant change since you last reviewed your finances.

After you have calculated your net worth, write down how much it is to-date.

Today: _____ (date).

My Assets (what I own) are:	
My Liabilities (what I owe) are:	
My total net worth is:	

Create Your Financial Goals

Now that you have a clear view of where you are financially, it's time for you to determine where you want to be. Consider this question: What one financial goal would you like to achieve over the next 12 months? Or look at it from this perspective as well: Considering your life goals, what financial progress will you need to make in the following year to make them happen?

Also, review the previous decisions you have made in this workbook. Re-examine what you calculated for income, tithing, saving, investing, living expenses (spending), giving, and debt reduction. These are financial goals that you may want to include in your worksheet.

Please dream a little here. You know your financial position, so you have an idea of what you can achieve a year from now. If you have more than one financial goal and you believe you can handle it, go ahead and write them down, but I suggest that you stick to 2 or 3 goals for now since you're just planning a year ahead.

If you think you need to learn more about setting SMART but FAITH goals before proceeding, you can refer to the *Make Your Year A Living Success Goals Workbook* (https://www.amazon.com/gp/product/0991785037/) or my website www.pamelavcarmichael.com for more on information.

My No.1 Financial Goal

Start Date: _____

End date: _____

By this end date I will know that I have made financial progress because:

_____

_____

_____

_____

_____

_____

_____

My No.2 Financial Goal

Start Date: _____

End date: _____

By this end date I will know that I have made financial progress because:

_____

_____

_____

_____

_____

_____

The aim of the **Financial Goals Worksheet** in the next exercise is to include the important goals for a year (or whatever period you choose to work with e.g. 90-days) on one page. Why? To give you a one-page vision of what you are targeting. Remember, consider what you want to achieve, not only from a financial perspective but with your life. Some of your life goals can have an impact on your finances or your finances can have an impact on them. Either way you look at it, setting your financial goals requires you to consider your goals in other key areas: spiritual, family, physical, personal development (intellectual), social, career, and business.

Take action on the financial goals worksheet. Enter your financial position and the few specific goals you want to achieve. Write in note form how you think you will be able to achieve those goals—saving more, reducing cost, earning more. As you do this, think about how these goals will impact your cash flow.

My Financial Goals Worksheet

DESCRIPTION *Hint >*	What do I have now? *Access your current net worth*	What do I want in the next ____ months? *Focus on 2 - 3 money areas that are linked to your life goals*	How do I afford this? • *Save specific amount* • *Increase income* • *Reduce spending*
ASSETS			
Long term assets:			
Real Estate #1			
Real Estate #2			
Vehicle			
Other long-term asset			
Investments:			
Golden Years Savings #1			
Golden Years savings #2			
Brokerage Account #1			
Brokerage Account #2			
Other Investments			
Other Assets:			
Jewellery			
Personal Effects			
Household Items (e.g. appliances)			

DESCRIPTION Hint >	What do I have now? Access your current net worth	What do I want in the next ____ months? Focus on 2 - 3 money areas that are linked to your life goals	How do I afford this? • Save specific amount • Increase income • Reduce spending
Liquid Accounts:			
Checking Account			
Emergency Fund – Freedom Fund			
Special Savings – Specific Goal			
Money Market			
TOTAL ASSETS			
LIABILITIES			
Long-term debt:			
Mortgage			
Car Loan			
Student Loan			
Other Loans			
Short-term debt:			
Credit Card #1			
Credit Card #2			
Line of Credit			
Other Debt			

DESCRIPTION *Hint >*	What do I have now? *Access your current net worth*	What do I want in the next _____ months? *Focus on 2 - 3 money areas that are linked to your life goals*	How do I afford this? • *Save specific amount* • *Increase income* • *Reduce spending*
TOTAL LIABILITIES			
NET WORTH			

With these your financial goals laid out on one page, make an effort to review them on a regular basis. Make sure to question your actions by asking yourself if you are getting closer to or further away from the goals you've set. Then adjust as needed.

Setup Your Financial Calendar

Your goals and life events are often linked to your finances. There are specific dates you will have in mind for attaining certain goals. There are also specific life events that matter to you as well. In both cases, money might be involved. The reality is that most goals or life events like birthdays, anniversaries, graduations, etc. often incur a cost. Hopefully, not all of your financial activity will have a negative effect on your financial position. I hope that some of your financial activity will produce financial increase.

In setting up your financial calendar, you will have a date visual of your goals and special life events for the year. You can even note an estimated dollar value (negative or positive), if your desire. I suggest that your first step should be marking the calendar with all the life events for the year e.g. birthdays, anniversaries, special occasions, vacation time, etc. Whatever important dates are known to you now, include them so that you can plan with them in mind. For your next step, add the dates for your financial and other life goals.

My Financial Calendar

Consider the following financial activities you can complete during the year. Not all of these may apply to you, but this list can give you some direction as to the type of money activity you need to consider throughout the year.

In the list below, next to each activity indicate those that apply to you and if there is a dollar amount involved. Then set up a reminder to address these before the due date in your calendar. Of course, add them to your spending plan.

While considering these activities, you look at other possible cash activity that can have an impact on your cash flow and your financial goals overall. Think about these kinds of events:

- Unexpected events – vehicle repairs, house maintenance, sickness or accident
- Ad-hoc expenses – annual insurance premiums (e.g. vehicle or property), property taxes, income tax return payments, etc.
- Celebration expenses – birthdays, anniversaries, vacation, travel costs and other special occasions

Month & Associated Activity	Applicable to me? Income or Cost amount?	Due date
JANUARY		
Set financial goals e.g. savings goals (Freedom Fund, Golden Years, Child Education, Fun or Travel, Household / Big ticket items)		
Have a preliminary spending plan – remember important dates like insurance premiums, tax instalments, etc.		
Prepare drop box for ongoing bills		

Organize other files e.g. permanent docs		
Set up spreadsheet or other program for recording money activity		
Review financial plan and update as needed		
Make sure all family members are on board with updated plan and knows when important documents are kept		
FEBRUARY		
Compile income tax info		
If needed, contact and make an appointment with the tax preparer		
Review your credit report and address any discrepancies		
MARCH		
Perform a quarterly review and make any necessary adjustments		
Too much debt? Make a plan to reduce it, see a debt counsellor or money coach for extra advise and support		
Assess your life goals against your financial activity. Do they match up? Adjust as needed.		

Review your mindset too – has your perspective on money matters shifted? Are they aligning with God's will? Have you been thinking negatively? Have you been praying about your finances as you do other areas of your life?		
APRIL		
Complete and file Income tax before the deadline		
Have to pay taxes, consider how you will do that		
Are you expecting a tax refund? Consider saving it rather than spending it or use it to reduce any debts		
MAY		
Review deadlines of upcoming payments in the next few months. To keep track calendar reminders and/ or setup automated payment schedules online, if possible.		
JUNE		
Perform mid-year review and make any necessary adjustments		
If you have incurred additional debt (outside of your mortgage) consider readjusting your spending so you can pay them off		

Review your cash flow and make sure you are meeting your savings/investing goals		
JULY		
If there are travel or other vacation plans make sure you have sufficient funds in place for this or make a plan of how you will pay for it		
Remember, school is just around the corner, you should have an estimate of the back-to-school expenses in place		
Prepare for the summer/vacation season if you haven't already done so. Relax and enjoy it without over spending :).		
AUGUST		
Take a summer break or vacation from the money matters.		
SEPTEMBER		
Perform quarterly review and make any necessary adjustments		

Review your mind set too – has your perspective on money matters shifted? Are they aligning with God's will? Have you been thinking negatively? Have you been praying about your finances as you do other areas of your life?		
OCTOBER		
Consider setting up an account for the upcoming holiday season – make a gift list, set a spending limit		
NOVEMBER		
Get an early start on the gift shopping and likely save some money. Most items tend to cost more in the later part of the year.		
Before the annual review, look at your portfolio and rebalance if needed. A lot can happen in a short time, so consider portfolio and retirement account reviews quarterly.		
DECEMBER		
Make sure you have at least the minimum deductibles for tax purposes e.g. retirement account contributions, donations, etc.		

Determine if you've reached your financial goals and make any adjustments before year end. Celebrate the highs and even the lows and look forward to the new year with hope.		

Note: If you are the type to forget or there's just too much going on, consider adding these dates with a timely reminder to any electronic calendar.

Figure Out Your Cash Flow

You may think this is repetitive. If you have completed the section titled, **Complete a Spending Plan**, great! You've done some good work. However, considering that you have now set goals and completed a financial calendar, you might want to adjust your spending plan or cash flow.

For this exercise, please go back to **Complete a Spending Plan** section and readjust any figures as needed or create a new spending plan if your goals and living expenses have changed significantly. Please make sure that you have a positive cash flow at the end of each month. In other words, don't eat all your seed. Try to have a positive cash balance. If there is a need to cover additional or unexpected expenses (that are below what your Freedom Fund ('Emergency' Savings) account), you might be able to cover them from your normal cash flow.

This spending plan or estimated cash flow is your reference guide for your financial activity through the year or whatever period you choose to work with (e.g. 90 days). Therefore, there should be room for flexibility, as life does not always go as planned.

If you are keen at using spreadsheets for this process, you may want to take the cash flow and convert it to a register with the following headings.

Day	Date	Description	Incoming	Outgoing	Balance	Comments

This will give you an even better overview of your financial activity since you can calculate a running balance of your checking account. Once per year, I create an estimate cash flow of my checking account.

Ongoing Financial Maintenance

After creating an estimated cash flow, you will need to review and update on a regular basis. Once a week (or every two weeks), you can update the spreadsheet with the actual activity and recalculate for upcoming income and expenses. This will give you a bird's eye view of your account ahead of time. You will see if you are heading into overdraft, or if you have enough to cover all your upcoming living expenses. Furthermore, you can make adjustments before you run into financial difficulty. This might prove to be the tool that will keep you out of the red and always in the black!

Along with the cash flow statement of your living expenses (i.e. checking activity), you might want to consider creating worksheets to monitor your savings account or investments accounts. Furthermore, within the same workbook, each quarter you will need to update your financial position worksheet to see how you are progressing. If you like using spreadsheets you might even want to create charts to show you an overview in a more visual format.

However, I can understand that this is a manual and a time-consuming process. If you prefer to and think a more automated process will work for you, consider carefully investing in a personal finance software that will help you monitor all your financial activity.

Whatever you do, please keep up the good work of managing your finances. I want you to experience financial empowerment!

PRAYING ABOUT YOUR FINANCES

God's word is living and active. It is sharper than any two-edged sword and cuts as deep as the place where soul and spirit meet, the place where joints and marrow meet. God's word judges a person's thoughts and intentions." — Hebrews 4:12 (GW)

This workbook was created with the Christian in mind. As such, I cannot end this without reiterating the importance of God and His word to your success in life and in your finances. As the scripture verse above shows, God's word is alive, active and definitely powerful. When you know God's heart is concerning you and your life, you become more confident in your approach to handling finances and your life.

Whether I am dealing with money matters or other life challenges, I make every effort to delve into the word of God to learn how to align them to God's plans or purpose for my life. We have always heard that there is a Word for every situation in our lives. God is always speaking and His word is one avenue by which He speaks to you and me.

Below is a list of scripture verses along with a declaration or prayer which covers the key areas of personal finance covered in this workbook. I encourage you to take from this list and from your Bible research key verses that speak to your specific circumstance right now. Maybe you are in deep debt—apply a few doses of God's word regarding debt to help you through the journey to reducing that debt or become debt free altogether. Maybe you are in need of a financial increase— consider the cost of living increases you've been experiencing, then search the Bible to find out how God can provide for you and trust His word.

Let these scriptures be a part of your prayer strategy. As you pray consistently in these life areas, anticipate positive change. God will give you direction regarding specific money or life matters and He who is faithful will answer your prayers.

Know God's Word About Money

Below is a list of scriptures that you can use as a starting point to understanding what God has to say about your money. You can add more verses to this list since there are over 2,500 references to money found in the Bible. You may even find quotations by Christian leaders that speak about money which resonate with you.

The goal of this exercise is to renew your mind with God's word. Highlight any verses that stand out for you and pray the Word daily. I have taken the liberty to add a declaration or short prayer that relates to each verse.

Prayer the Word and experience the power of God at work transforming your life. When you pray according to the word, this kind of prayer moves you from concentrating on what is wrong in your life to seeing life from God's perspective and life in agreement with His will.

God's Word	My Declaration or Prayer
"Therefore do not worry, saying, 'What shall we eat?' or 'What shall we drink?' or 'What shall we wear?' For after all these things the Gentiles seek. For your heavenly Father knows that you need all these things. But seek first the kingdom of God and His righteousness, and all these things shall be added to you." — Matthew 6:31-33	When I put God FIRST in my life, all my needs are supplied. I don't need to worry.
"The rich rules over the poor, and the borrower is servant to the lender" — Proverbs 22:7	I am a lender.
"For the Lord your God will bless you just as He promised you; you shall lend to many nations, but you shall not borrow; you shall reign over many nations, but they shall not reign over you." — Deuteronomy 15:6	I will lend and not borrow.
"Where there is no counsel, the people fall; but in the multitude of counselors there is safety." — Proverbs 11:14 *"Without counsel, plans go awry, but in the multitude of counselors they are established."* — Proverbs 15:22	I will seek wise counsel.

God's Word	My Declaration or Prayer
"If any of you lacks wisdom, let him ask of God, who gives to all liberally and without reproach, and it will be given to him." — James 1:5	Lord, give me financial wisdom.
"For you know the grace of our Lord Jesus Christ, that though He was rich, yet for your sakes He became poor, that you through His poverty might become rich." — 2 Corinthians 8:9	Christ died poor so I would become rich.
"But his delight is in the law of the Lord, and in His law he meditates day and night. He shall be like a tree planted by the rivers of water, that brings forth its fruit in its season, whose leaf also shall not wither; and whatever he does shall prosper." — Psalm 1:2–3	I will find pleasure in God's law and because I do this I will prosper in whatever I do.
"And you shall remember the Lord your God, for it is He who gives you power to get wealth, that He may establish His covenant which He swore to your fathers, as it is this day." — Deuteronomy 8:18	The Lord my God gives me the anointing to attain wealth. He gives me creative ability to get wealth and to distribute it where needed.
"For exaltation comes neither from the east nor from the west nor from the south. But God is the Judge: He puts down one, and exalts another." — Psalm 75:6–7	God will promote me.

God's Word	My Declaration or Prayer
"Bring all the tithes into the storehouse, that there may be food in My house, and try Me now in this,' says the Lord of hosts, 'If I will not open for you the windows of heaven and pour out for you such blessing that there will not be room enough to receive it. And I will rebuke the devourer for your sakes, so that he will not destroy the fruit of your ground, nor shall the vine fail to bear fruit for you in the field,' says the Lord of hosts; 'And all nations will call you blessed, for you will be a delightful land,' says the Lord of hosts." — Malachi 3:10–12	As I tithe God will pour out blessings on me beyond measure.
"And God is able to make all grace abound toward you, that you, always having all sufficiency in all things, may have an abundance for every good work." —2 Corinthians 9:8	God's grace will abound towards me and provide me with more than enough to do good works.
"Go to the ant, you sluggard! Consider her ways and be wise, which, having no captain, overseer or ruler, provides her supplies in the summer, and gathers her food in the harvest." — Proverbs 6:6–8	I am wise to save and invest.
"The Lord will command the blessing on you in your storehouses and in all to which you set your hand, and He will bless you in the land which the Lord your God is giving you." — Deuteronomy 28:8	The Lord will command the blessing on my savings and investments and bless me in the place where I live.
"A good man leaves an inheritance to his children's children, but the wealth of the sinner is stored up for the righteous." — Proverbs 13:22	As a righteous child of God, I will leave an inheritance for my future generations.

God's Word	My Declaration or Prayer
"The Lord will open to you His good treasure, the heavens, to give the rain to your land in its season, and to bless all the work of your hand. You shall lend to many nations, but you shall not borrow." — Deuteronomy 28:12	I receive from the open heavens God's supply for me and his blessing on what I do.
"And my God will liberally supply (fill to the full) your every need according to His riches in glory in Christ Jesus." — Philippians 4:19 (AMP)	The Lord will abundantly supply, copiously supply, adequately supply, and sufficiently supply all my needs.
"The Lord is my Shepherd [to feed, guide, and shield me], I shall not lack." — Psalm. 23:1 (AMP)	I will not lack anything good thing because the Lord is my Shepherd who feeds, guides and shields me.
"The fear of the Lord is the beginning of knowledge, but fools despise wisdom and instruction." — Proverbs 1:7 "The fear of the Lord is the beginning of wisdom, and the knowledge of the Holy One is understanding." — Proverbs 9:10	I have the fear of the Lord and therefore I have knowledge and wisdom to live a good life.
"Give, and it will be given to you: good measure, pressed down, shaken together, and running over will be put into your bosom. For with the same measure that you use, it will be measured back to you." — Luke 6:38	When I give, I receive more in super abundance.

My Financial Empowerment Prayer Strategy

In the space provided below, you can write out your own prayer concerning your finances. In all things remember to give God **takes**, ask for help where you need His help and be quick to repent in areas where you have fallen. God is a loving God and a gracious Father who desires the best for His children. Be open to Him and follow His lead. Blessings.

_____

_____

CONGRATULATIONS!

Way to go! You're on the Road to Financial Empowerment

Congrats on a job well done! If you have come to the end of this workbook having completed the exercises or action steps, I applaud you. And God is smiling at you too!

I must say that writing this workbook has not been anything short of challenging. I have written and re-written quite a few times hoping to capture the essence of what God wants you to understand about money and ultimately your relationship with Him. I hope that I have been able to do justice (so to speak) with this work God has commissioned me to do.

My desire is that you gather much good out of this Financial Empowerment Workbook experience and that you continue to develop your financial management skills. This certainly is a road less travelled, but one that is well worth the time and effort.

Thank you again for your support. Yes, your support. Although you benefit greatly from this workbook, I do also. As I receive your emails and testimonies of how God has used this workbook and the book (for those who have read it) I am encouraged to continue learning and writing so I can share more with you.

If you need further assistance, you can contact me via www.pamelavcarmichael.com. I offer the Financial Empowerment Coaching Program which is geared specifically to your needs and provides a greater level of accountability to assist you in achieving your goals.

Once again, congrats in completing this workbook.

To your Financial Empowerment!

Pamela Carmichael

PLEASE SHARE YOUR EXPERIENCE

Write a Review

One more thing before you go.

Seeing that you have reached the end of this book, I can only conclude that you liked what you have read and it was beneficial to you. At least I hope so. ☺

Please leave a review for this book on Amazon. I'd really appreciate it. Your review would not only help others decide if this book is right for them, but it will help sell more books. This will in turn assist me in writing more books for you.

To leave a review, go to https://www.amazon.com/, search for the book page: The Financial Empowerment Workbook by Pamela Carmichae. Scroll down the page and click on the 'Write a customer review' button. From there you can select the star rating and write a short note about your experience with this book. If you used a different platform, by all means you can leave a review there too!

Thank you for reading, and thank you so much for being part of this journey with me.

You can also share what you have gained from this workbook with your family and friends so that they can experience some of the value and take advantage of it.

Share on Social Media

I'd also like to hear from you. It's encouraging to authors when readers comment about their work. So send me a Tweet or Facebook post. I am looking forward to hearing from you!
You can also connect with me via any other of these social media platforms.

https://www.facebook.com/PamelaVCarmichaelAuthor

https://plus.google.com/+PamelaCarmichael

https://twitter.com/PamvCarmichael

http://www.pamelavcarmichael.com

NOTES

ADDITIONAL RESOURCES FROM PAMELA

In this award-winning title, *Financial Empowerment: Realign Your Finances to God's Will*, Pamela explores nine key areas of personal finance:- creating wealth, tithing, saving, giving, investing, spending, borrowing, lending and planning. She examines the issues and misconceptions most experience in their finances and provides help with Biblical and practical solutions.

Financial Empowerment is the road map to personal and spiritual growth, financial well-being and a lifetime of empowerment through Godly principles.

Get your copy at https://www.amazon.com/

Pamela Carmichael is a passionate educator of financial empowerment for people. She produces workshops and seminars centred on financial literacy education.

Learn more at http://www.pamelavcarmichael.com/speaking/

PAMELA CARMICHAEL: AUTHOR | SPEAKER | COACH

Pamela Carmichael is a passionate educator of financial empowerment for people. Her Financial Empowerment Initiative produces workshops and seminars centred on financial literacy education. Pamela is concerned about the general lack of fundamental and basic financial education of both youth and adults. Pamela combines her passion to see others succeed with her 18+ years' experience in the financial services industry to train others to effectively manage their finances. Her concern for those who struggle financially has led her to authoring the award-winning book titled *Financial Empowerment: Re-align Your Finances to God's Will*.

Pamela's desire to deliver quality financial education inspired her to gain the Certified Financial Education Instructor (National Financial Education Council) designation. She is also a member of the Personal Finance Speakers Association. Pamela conducts financial empowerment workshops, speaking events, money life coaching programs to help people move from financial struggle to success and significance. She also shares insights on her Living Success blog relating to managing your personal finances and to living successfully through the study and application of God's word. Pamela has a Bachelor's degree in Economics & Accounting (University of the West Indies Cave Hill Campus) and has a successful career as a financial service professional with over 18 years' experience. Along with her financial education certification, she is also a Certified Professional Coach (Wainwright Global, Inc.; Institute of Professional Coaching) and a Success Principles Certified Coach.

An author, a teacher, an encourager, a coach and more, Pamela combines her passion for financial empowerment along with her experience and training in financial services, financial education and life coaching to educate and motivate people to take action toward achieving financial freedom and personal success that multiplies into positive changes in society.

Connect with Pamela:

https://www.facebook.com/PamelaVCarmichaelAuthor

https://plus.google.com/+PamelaCarmichael

https://twitter.com/PamvCarmichael

http://www.pamelavcarmichael.com